First World War
and Army of Occupation
War Diary
France, Belgium and Germany

40 DIVISION
120 Infantry Brigade,
Brigade Machine Gun Company
15 June 1916 - 28 February 1918

WO95/2612/4

The Naval & Military Press Ltd
www.nmarchive.com
Published in association with The National Archives

Published by

The Naval & Military Press Ltd

Unit 10 Ridgewood Industrial Park,
Uckfield, East Sussex,
TN22 5QE England
Tel: +44 (0) 1825 749494

www.naval-military-press.com
www.nmarchive.com

Contents

Document type	Place/Title	Date From	Date To
Heading	WO95/2612 (4)		
Heading	40th Division 120th Infy Bde 120th Machine Gun Coy. Jun 1916-Feb 1918.		
Heading	War Diary 120 Machine Gun Company. June 15th 1916.		
War Diary	Grantham	15/06/1916	16/06/1916
War Diary	Southampton	16/06/1916	16/06/1916
War Diary	Havre.	17/06/1916	19/06/1916
War Diary	Bruay.	20/06/1916	29/06/1916
Heading	War Diary Of 120th Machine Gun Company Fro 1.7.16 to 31.7.16. Vol 2.		
War Diary	Bruay.	01/07/1916	30/07/1916
Operation(al) Order(s)	Operation Order No. 5. Appendix 2.		
Operation(al) Order(s)	Operation Order No. 6. Appendix 3.		
Operation(al) Order(s)	Operation Order No. 8.	21/07/1916	21/07/1916
Operation(al) Order(s)	Operation Order No. 9. Appendix 5.	28/07/1916	28/07/1916
Heading	War Diary of 120th Machine Gun Company Aug 1916.		
War Diary	Grenay.	01/08/1916	04/08/1916
War Diary	Grenay (Company in trench in Loos Sector)	05/08/1916	09/08/1916
War Diary	Grenay (Coy in trench in Maroc Sector)	10/08/1916	11/08/1916
War Diary	Grenay.	12/08/1916	31/08/1916
Operation(al) Order(s)	Operation Order No. 19. Appendix	03/06/1916	03/06/1916
Operation(al) Order(s)	Operation Order No. 12. Appendix No. 7.	09/08/1916	09/08/1916
Operation(al) Order(s)	Operation Order No. 13. Appendix No. 8	05/08/1916	05/08/1916
Operation(al) Order(s)	Operation Order No. 14. Appendix No. 9		
Heading	War Diary of 120th Machine Gun Company September 1916.		
War Diary	Grenay.	01/09/1916	11/09/1916
War Diary	Grenay to Les Brebis	12/09/1916	12/09/1916
War Diary	Les Brebis.	13/09/1916	16/09/1916
War Diary	Grenay to Les Brebis	12/09/1916	12/09/1916
War Diary	Les Brebis.	13/09/1916	21/09/1916
War Diary	Les Brebis to Mazincarbe.	23/09/1916	23/09/1916
War Diary	Malingarbe.	24/09/1916	30/09/1916
Heading	War Diary 120 Machine Gun Company October 1916. Vol 5.		
War Diary	Mazingarbe (Coy H.q.s) 14 Bis Section Trenches.	01/10/1916	06/10/1916
War Diary	Mazingarbe	06/10/1916	10/10/1916
War Diary	Mazingabe to Philosophe.	11/10/1916	11/10/1916
War Diary	14 Bis to Hulluch Sector.	11/10/1916	13/10/1916
War Diary	Philosophe Trenches in Hulluch Secton.	14/10/1916	24/10/1916
War Diary	Les Brebis to Bruay	25/10/1916	26/10/1916
War Diary	Orlencourt.	28/10/1916	28/10/1916
War Diary	Ocoche.	29/10/1916	31/10/1916
Operation(al) Order(s)	120th Infantry Brigade Order No. 39.	25/10/1916	25/10/1916
Miscellaneous	March Table To Accompany 120th Infantry Brigade Operation Order No. 41.		
Operation(al) Order(s)	120th Infantry Brigade Operation Order No. 41.	28/10/1916	28/10/1916
Miscellaneous	March Table To Accompany 120th Infantry Brigade Operation Order No. 40.		

Map			
Operation(al) Order(s)	120th Infantry Brigade Operation Order No. 40.	26/10/1916	26/10/1916
Miscellaneous			
Miscellaneous	March Table To Accompany 120th Infantry Brigade O.O. No. 39.		
Miscellaneous			
Miscellaneous	H.2. 120 Inf Bde.		
War Diary	Ocoche to Sibiville.	01/11/1916	02/11/1916
War Diary	Noeux to St. Hilaire.	04/11/1916	11/11/1916
War Diary	Doullens to Bayencourt.	12/11/1916	15/11/1916
War Diary	Hebuterne.	16/11/1916	20/11/1916
War Diary	Coigneux to Orville.	21/11/1916	22/11/1916
War Diary	Berneuil To Gorenflos.	24/11/1916	24/11/1916
War Diary	Gorenflos To Alliel	25/11/1916	30/11/1916
Miscellaneous	March Table To Accompany 120th Infantry Brigade Operation Order No. 43.		
Miscellaneous	March Table To Accompany 120th Infantry Brigade Operation Order No. 44.		
Miscellaneous	March Table To Accompany 120th Infantry Brigade Operation Order No. 45.		
Miscellaneous	March Table To Accompany 120th Infantry Brigade Operation Order No. 48.		
Miscellaneous	Programme To Accompany 120th Infantry Brigade Operation Order No. 49.		
Miscellaneous	March Table To Accompany 120th Infantry Brigade Operation Order No. 54.		
Operation(al) Order(s)	120th Infantry Brigade Operation Order No. 53.	19/11/1916	19/11/1916
Operation(al) Order(s)	120th Infantry Brigade Order No. 57.	25/11/1916	25/11/1916
Miscellaneous	March Table To Accompany 120th Inf. Bde. Order No. 56.		
Miscellaneous	March Table To Accompany 120th Infantry Brigade Order No. 65.		
War Diary	Alliel.	01/12/1916	31/12/1916
Heading	War Diary of 120th Machine Gun Company Volume 8. January 1917. Vol 8.		
War Diary	Suzanne.	01/01/1917	03/01/1917
War Diary	Rancourt.	04/01/1917	11/01/1917
War Diary	Suzanne.	12/01/1917	19/01/1917
War Diary	Bouchavesnes North.	19/01/1917	26/01/1917
War Diary	Corbie.	27/01/1917	31/01/1917
War Diary		30/01/1917	30/01/1917
War Diary	Corbie.	01/02/1917	15/02/1917
Heading	War Diary of 120th Machine Gun Company Vol 10. Feb 16th March 31st 1917. Vol 10.		
War Diary	Camp 112.	16/02/1917	22/02/1917
War Diary	Rancourt Sector.	23/02/1917	05/03/1917
War Diary	Camp 21 Suzanne.	05/03/1917	06/03/1917
War Diary	Bethune Road Sector.	07/03/1917	22/03/1917
War Diary	Hem Wood Locality.	23/03/1917	31/03/1917
Miscellaneous	Headquarters 120th Inf Bde.	17/03/1917	17/03/1917
Operation(al) Order(s)	120th Infantry Brigade Order No. 81.	15/03/1917	15/03/1917
Miscellaneous			
War Diary	Dug-Outs Near Hem Wood (Map Ref. 62. C.N.W. 1:20,000 H.3.C)	01/04/1919	05/04/1919
War Diary	Dus Outs W Hem Wood.	06/04/1917	11/04/1917
War Diary	Nera Hem Wood.	11/04/1917	12/04/1917

War Diary	Equancourt.	13/04/1917	30/04/1917
Heading	War Diary of 120 Machine Gun Company Volume 12: May 1917. Vol. 12.		
War Diary	Dessart Wood 57 C.S.E. 1/20,000 W.1.a.9.2.	01/05/1917	04/05/1917
War Diary	Dessart Wood.	04/05/1917	12/05/1917
War Diary	Heudecourt.	12/05/1917	12/05/1917
War Diary	Ref 57. C.S.E. W.12.b.6.9.	13/05/1917	17/05/1917
War Diary	W.12.b.6.9.	18/05/1917	31/05/1917
War Diary	W.b.d.6.0.	01/06/1917	10/06/1917
War Diary	Dessart Wood W.1.b.9.1.	11/06/1917	18/06/1917
War Diary	Q.9.6.2.0. (Sheet 57.C.S.E.2).	19/06/1917	24/06/1917
War Diary	Q.29.b.2.0.	24/06/1917	30/06/1917
War Diary	Q.29.b.2.0. (57. C.S.E.2).	01/07/1917	10/07/1917
War Diary	Q.29.b.2.0.	11/07/1917	14/07/1917
War Diary	Q.29.b.2.0. (57. C.S.E.2).	15/07/1917	31/07/1917
War Diary	Caesar's Camp.	01/08/1917	01/08/1917
War Diary	Q.29.b.2.0. (57. C.S.E.2).	02/08/1917	02/08/1917
War Diary	Q.8.b.70.90.	03/08/1917	12/08/1917
War Diary	Q.8.b.7.9.	13/08/1917	07/09/1917
War Diary	Heudecourt.	07/09/1917	21/09/1917
War Diary	Q.12.d.60.0.5	22/09/1917	22/09/1917
War Diary	Couzeaucourt 1/20,000.	22/09/1917	25/09/1917
War Diary	Q.12.d.60.0.5.	26/09/1917	28/09/1917
War Diary	Gouzeaucourt 1/20,000.	29/09/1917	30/09/1917
War Diary	Q.12.d.60.05. Rd Gouzeaucourt 1/20,000.	01/10/1917	05/10/1917
War Diary	Heudecourt.	05/10/1917	06/10/1917
War Diary	Peronne.	07/10/1917	09/10/1917
War Diary	Berneville.	10/10/1917	28/10/1917
War Diary	Pohera.	29/10/1917	31/10/1917
War Diary	Walincourt.	01/11/1917	15/11/1917
War Diary	Walincourt Berneville.	16/11/1917	16/11/1917
War Diary	Berneville & Courcelles le Court.	17/11/1917	17/11/1917
War Diary	Courcelles Le Comte	18/11/1917	19/11/1917
War Diary	Boulencourt.	20/11/1917	21/11/1917
War Diary	Lebuquerie.	22/11/1917	22/11/1917
War Diary	In The Field.	23/11/1917	30/11/1917
Miscellaneous	H.Q. 120th Inf. Bde.	31/12/1917	31/12/1917
War Diary	Hutments Hendercourt Les Ranzart (Len 1/10,0000.I, IV).	01/12/1917	03/12/1917
War Diary	Moyne Camp Moyenneville (Lens 1d. 1/100000 J, IV.)	04/12/1917	04/12/1917
War Diary	93 Shaft Trench T.6.a.30.70.	05/12/1917	08/12/1917
War Diary	93 Shaft Trench T.6.a.30.70. (Trench Map Bullecourt 51.B S.W.4).	09/12/1917	10/12/1917
War Diary	St. Leger.	11/12/1917	19/12/1917
War Diary	McYne Camp Noyneville.	20/12/1917	23/12/1917
War Diary	St. Leger.	24/12/1917	26/12/1917
War Diary	Moyne Camp.	27/12/1917	27/12/1917
War Diary	Moreuil.	28/12/1917	15/01/1918
War Diary	Dysart Camp Ervillers.	16/01/1918	22/01/1918
War Diary	Noreuil.	22/01/1918	11/02/1918
War Diary	Durrow camp. Mory.	12/02/1918	12/02/1918
War Diary	Hendecourt Lez Ransart.	13/02/1918	19/02/1918
War Diary	Ervillers.	20/02/1918	28/02/1918

WO95/2612(4)

WO95/2612(4)

40TH DIVISION
120TH INFY BDE

120TH MACHINE GUN COY.

JUN 1916-FEB 1918

120 M G Coy
Vol 1
June

WAR DIARY.

XL

120. MACHINE GUN COMPANY.

A. Travers Lacey Capt.

O.C.
120. M.G. COY.

JUNE . 15th 1916 - - - -

Instructions regarding War Diaries and Intelligence Summaries are contained in F. S. Regs., Part II. and the Staff Manual respectively. Title Pages will be prepared in manuscript.

O. M.G. COY.

WAR DIARY
or
~~INTELLIGENCE SUMMARY~~
(Erase heading not required.)

Army Form C. 2118. P1.

120 MACHINE GUN COMPANY
MACHINE GUN CORPS

Place	Date	Hour	Summary of Events and Information	Remarks and references to Appendices
GRANTHAM	15-6-16 / 16-6-16	12 midnight	The Coy entrained at MILITARY DOCK.	
SOUTHAMPTON	16.6.16	9.45 AM.	Arrived SOUTHAMPTON. R.T.O had not been informed of correct establishment, & had to obtain permission for 2nd in Command and 2 O.R. to proceed.	
"	"	8. P.M.	½ Coy under C.O, with all Transport sailed in S.S. COURTLAND. } Neither boat had wireless installed.	
		8.30 "	½ Coy under 2nd in C. sailed in S.S. CAESAREA. }	
			Learnt afterwards that during night one of our transport boats rammed and sank destroyer.	
HAVRE	17-6-16	7. A.M.	2nd in Command and party disembarked.	
		11.30 "	O.C and party disembarked. Method of disembarking animals as directed by M.L.O seemed bad. Animals of all units on board were driven - not led - pell mell down gangways: many fell - others lost shoes and there was great confusion on the quay as each driver was pushing about to see when his own animal was coming. G.S. Waggon attached to Coy from this time.	
		6. P.M (18 hours)	Coy arrived at No 1 REST CAMP HAVRE.	
	18-6-16	9. P.M (21 hours)	½ Coy under C.O. entrained with 119 M.G. Coy. arrived ABBEVILLE 12 hours 19-6-16 BRUAY (5½ miles S.W BETHUNE) 18.10 hours	
		9.30 (21.30 hours)	½ " 2nd in C " 121 " " " 12.30 " " 18.40 hours	
	19.6.16		Coy went into billets BRUAY.	

2449 Wt. W14957/M90 750,000 1/16 J.B.C. & A. Forms/C.2118/12.

Army Form C. 2118.

Instructions regarding War Diaries and Intelligence Summaries are contained in F. S. Regs., Part II. and the Staff Manual respectively. Title Pages will be prepared in manuscript.

120. M.G. COY.

WAR DIARY
or
~~INTELLIGENCE SUMMARY~~

(Erase heading not required.)

Place	Date	Hour	Summary of Events and Information	Remarks and references to Appendices
BRUAY.	20-6-16.		Difficulty experienced in rations as S.O. HAVRE had only issued one days ration instead of two. Two men to be detailed as permanent fatigue for unloading to A.S.C. – result company loses two gun numbers: first sign of insufficient personnel.	
"	22-6-16	14.30	Inspection of M.G. Coys of 40th Div. by General Munro G.O.C. 1st Army.	
"	24-6-16	8.	O.C. Coy 4 Section officers and 10 N.C.Os left BRUAY and proceed to VERMELLES for instruction in trench warfare being attached to 45th Bde. M.G. Coy. 4 Section officers & 10 N.C.Os	
	25-6-16		returned BRUAY on 25th & 2nd in Command and 3 Sub. section officers took their place.	
	26.6.16.		O.C. Coy & this party left VERMELLES at 11 hours on 26th. No casualties during instruction. 45th Bde M.G Coy had several men attached to them from the Infantry battalions and one extra officer as they had found the personnel quite insufficient. They had been out since February 1916 and had only ~~had~~ had about 6 casualties though they had been in the LOOS SALIENT & HOHENZOLLERN SECTOR most of the time. They had 10 guns in front line – 3 in support – remainder in reserve or village lines. Telephone communication to Bde Hqrs only, owing to small number of signallers (4) allowed in War Establishment.	
BRUAY	27.6.16		Arranged with Brigade to train 25 men from each Inf. Battn (see appendix 1.) in Vickers & Lewis Gun: to supervise training of 3rd Sections in turn: Each battalion	

Instructions regarding War Diaries and Intelligence Summaries are contained in F. S. Regs., Part II, and the Staff Manual respectively. Title Pages will be prepared in manuscript.

120. M.G. COY.

WAR DIARY
or
~~INTELLIGENCE SUMMARY~~

(Erase heading not required.)

1

Army Form C. 2118. 3

Place	Date	Hour	Summary of Events and Information	Remarks and references to Appendices
			had tried to train 4 sections: 1st & 2nd were the "Service" Sections and 3 & 4 the extra ones. It was the fourth that was to be trained by me in order to have extra men for my Company to replace casualties till reinforcements were received. As the number of Lewis Automatic rifles would probably be increased to 8 per infantry battalion both 1 & 2 sections would be needed & the reserve officers. The 3rd section was to replace casualties in the "Service" Sections & the 4th to replace casualties in both battalion & Brigade Machine Gunners.	
	29-6-16		Party consisting of 2 officers from each battalion & O.C. & 1 officer from our Company reconnoitred reserve line of 142nd Bde which was in a sector with headquarters at AIX NOULETTE (Ref. map 1/20,000 FRANCE SHEET 36B. S.E. R. 22.) The line had no M.G. emplacements & did not exist at all in some places e.g. in the BOIS DE NOULETTE. The Brigade had come recently from the VIMY SECTOR & said their present position was a far more comfortable one.	
			General	
			During period 20 - 30th of the month the Company was in billets at BRUAY continuing its training special attention being paid to overhead & indirect fire: certain equipment which was not issued in ENGLAND was obtained though lock springs could not be got.	

O.C. 120. M.G. COY. [illegible] Capt.

2449 Wt. W14957/M90 750,000 1/16 J.B.C. & A. Forms/C.2118/12.

Instructions regarding War Diaries and Intelligence Summaries are contained in F. S. Regs., Part II. and the Staff Manual respectively. Title Pages will be prepared in manuscript.

120. M.G. COY.

WAR DIARY
or
INTELLIGENCE SUMMARY

(Erase heading not required.)

Army Form C. 2118. 4

Place	Date	Hour	Summary of Events and Information	Remarks and references to Appendices
	JUNE 1916.		FIRST ARMY.	APPENDIX 1.

FIRST ARMY.
- 1st CORPS
  - 40th DIV.
    - 119th Inf Bde
    - 120th Bde
      - 14th H.L.I.
      - 13. E SURREY.
      - 11. R LANCS.
      - 14th A.&S.H.
      - 120. M.G. Coy.
      - 120. T.M. Battery.
    - 121st Bde

2449 Wt. W14957/M90 750,000 1/16 J.B.C. & A. Forms/C.2118/12.

40 July

120 M.G.C.

Vol 2

CONFIDENTIAL.

War Diary

of

120th Machine Gun Company.

from. 1-7-16 to 31-7-16

VOL 2

Army Form C. 2118.

Instructions regarding War Diaries and Intelligence Summaries are contained in F. S. Regs., Part II. and the Staff Manual respectively. Title Pages will be prepared in manuscript.

WAR DIARY
or
~~INTELLIGENCE SUMMARY~~

(Erase heading not required.)

Place	Date	Hour	Summary of Events and Information	Remarks and references to Appendices
BRUAY	1.7.16		News received of Allied attack N. & S. of SOMME.	
"	2.7.16		Information received that 40th Div. were to relieve 1st Div. in CALONNE & MAROC Subsections. (R.20c – M.5.D)	
"	3.7.16		Operation orders from 120th Bde: the 120th Bde to relieve on the 4th the 3rd Bde who were in divisional reserve at LES BREBIS – the 3rd M.G. Coy being at GRENAY. Officer from Coy went to GRENAY to see reserve line of division – another officer to see billets of 3rd M.G. Coy: officer from 3rd M.G. Coy arrived at BRUAY for billets. 2/Lt Scott, batman, & 5 N.C.Os proceed on M.G. Course to 1st Army School at CAMIERES.	
	4.7.16.	5.45 am	Company started from BRUAY.	
		11 hrs.	Reached GRENAY via BARLIN and PETIT SAINS. Took over from 3rd Bde. M.G. Coy 2 guns of No 1 Section being in Reserve line at "Z" post (R.14.A.5.9). Coy. Hqs at house in GRENAY R.6.c.3.6.	
		12 hrs	3rd Bde. M.G. Coy leave GRENAY.	
		14 hrs.	Section officers go over RESERVE LINE & see emplacements to be occupied in case of alarm. The 3rd Bde M.G. Coy had a personnel of 275: when in the line it had 15 guns in for the Bde tour of 16 days: in view of this I made an application to Bde for extra men to be attached to my Coy otherwise it would be impossible to carry on system.	

2449 Wt. W14957/M90 750,000 1/16 J.B.C. & A. Forms/C.2118/12.

Army Form C. 2118.

WAR DIARY
or
~~INTELLIGENCE SUMMARY~~
(Erase heading not required.)

Instructions regarding War Diaries and Intelligence Summaries are contained in F. S. Regs., Part II. and the Staff Manual respectively. Title Pages will be prepared in manuscript.

Place	Date	Hour	Summary of Events and Information	Remarks and references to Appendices
GRENAY.	5-7-16		119th ~~M.G. Coy~~ Bde had relieved 2nd Bde in CALONNE SECTOR and 121st Bde the 1st Bde in MAROC SECTOR on 3rd & 4th inst. We reconnoitred the reserve line of the division and Section Officers & N.C.Os visited the emplacements they were to occupy in case of alarm.	
"	7-7-16		25 men from each battalion in the Brigade attached to Company – also 1 officer 2.Lt. HARDIE – 2nd Lewis Gun Officer of the H.L.I. Training of these started at once.	
"	8-7-16		The 2 guns of No1 Sect. in 2 post relieved by 2 guns of No2 Section.	
"	10-7-16 } 11-7-16 }		The MAROC SECTOR reconnoitred in view of fact that 120th Bde was to relieve the 121st Bde in this sector on the 12th instant.	
"	12-7-16		The Company relieved the 121st Bde M.G. Coy in MAROC SECTOR + Coy. Hqrs remains in same position. Two officers per section went up as this was our first tour – after two days one officer per section returned.	+ APPENDIX No. 2.
"	13-7-16		Quiet day in the trenches: little trench mortar activity.	
"	14-7-16		Situation normal. Enemy shelled our support and reserve lines from 14.40 – 15.40 hours. Our artillery retaliated.	

2449 Wt. W14957/M90 750,000 1/16 J.B.C. & A. Forms/C.2118/12.

Instructions regarding War Diaries and Intelligence Summaries are contained in F. S. Regs., Part II. and the Staff Manual respectively. Title Pages will be prepared in manuscript.

Army Form C. 2118.

WAR DIARY
or
~~INTELLIGENCE~~ SUMMARY
(Erase heading not required.)

Place	Date	Hour	Summary of Events and Information	Remarks and references to Appendices
	15.7.16		Quiet day. Our aeroplanes were active.	
	16.7.16		Rather more artillery fire and trench mortar activity.	
			2 N.C.Os sent on 3 days gas course.	
	17.7.16		Coy relieved by 121st M.G. Coy.* Infantry relieved next day. This tour was a quiet one - no casualties. Our machine guns were not very active owing to large number of working parties sent out by infantry. A little indirect fire was done each day.	*APPENDIX 3.
	18.7.16		Kit inspection and thorough cleaning of guns and spare parts ammunition etc.	
	19/20		Physical drill - drill with respirators & gas helmets. Training of attached men continued. CALONNE SECTOR reconnoitred.	
	20.7.16		Informed that Brigade was to relieve 119th Bde in CALONNE SECTOR on 22nd - machine guns to be relieved on 21st. Also that the 40th Div was extending its front to include LOOS SECTOR: the right brigade to hold from right of CALONNE SECTOR (map reference R.20.c.) to DOUBLE CRASSIER (M.4.c.)	

Instructions regarding War Diaries and Intelligence Summaries are contained in F. S. Regs., Part II. and the Staff Manual respectively. Title Pages will be prepared in manuscript.

WAR DIARY
or
~~INTELLIGENCE~~ SUMMARY
(Erase heading not required.)

Army Form C. 2118.

Place	Date	Hour	Summary of Events and Information	Remarks and references to Appendices
			Left Bde from DOUBLE CRASSIER salient to left of LOOS SECTOR.	
	21.7.16		Relieved 119 M.G. Coy in CALONNE SECTOR and took over four gun positions in Southern half of old MAROC SECTOR from 121st Bde*	* Appendix 4.
	22.7.16		Trenches and gun emplacements not so good as in MAROC Sector: enemy active with trench mortars especially near R.20.a.B.49. This locality is always being shelled by mortars and guns. 2 LT SCOTT and party return from CAMIERES	
	23.7.16		Situation quiet except for trench mortar activity. Our guns got a good opportunity on a working party at M.10.c.4.9. We also did indirect fire on enemy billets & communication trenches	
	24.7.16		Trench mortars very active again: also enemy's light field guns. Another working party of Germans dispersed. Indirect fire on billets continued.	
	25.7.16		2nd LT. HARDIE + 2 of attached N.C.O.S sent on VICKERS COURSE AT CAMIERES. Continued hostile trench mortar activity: indirect fire from our guns continued. Gaps in enemy wire caused by our mortars kept open by our guns.	

Instructions regarding War Diaries and Intelligence Summaries are contained in F. S. Regs., Part II. and the Staff Manual respectively. Title Pages will be prepared in manuscript.

WAR DIARY
or
~~INTELLIGENCE SUMMARY~~
(Erase heading not required.)

Army Form C. 2118.

Place	Date	Hour	Summary of Events and Information	Remarks and references to Appendices
	26.7.16		Quiet day.	
	27.7.16		Usual trench mortar activity. Our M. guns again did indirect fire and kept up during the night of 27-28th fire on gaps in enemy wire.	
	28.7.16		Internal relief of Company - both officers and men. Informed after this had taken place that we were to be relieved next day.	
	29.7.16		2Lt. BARRINGTON was accidentally shot and killed by one of ~~our~~ the sentries - our first casualty.	
			The Company was relieved by the 179th M. G. Coy.*	Appendix 5.
	30.7.16		In addition to having 2 guns in Z post - the reserve Company always supplied this - we had to put four guns in CALONNE defences.	
			GENERAL	
			For duty in the trenches normally we had 1 Officer and 2 N.C.O.S to four guns: 5 men to a gun team. With the extra two men we were enabled to have pioneers, police, men for service in the Coy. dry Canteen which was opened on 19-7-16, and also have sufficient men to relieve the gun teams in the trenches if necessary. As regards rations: these were packed in sandbags - two for	

Army Form C. 2118.

WAR DIARY
or
~~INTELLIGENCE~~ SUMMARY
(Erase heading not required.)

Instructions regarding War Diaries and Intelligence Summaries are contained in F. S. Regs., Part II. and the Staff Manual respectively. Title Pages will be prepared in manuscript.

Place	Date	Hour	Summary of Events and Information	Remarks and references to Appendices
			emplacement and sent up with the rations with transport. The men cooked for themselves in braziers. This was quite satisfactory. The officers in charge of sections reported twice daily to the C.O.s of battalions in whose sub sector they were also they visited the Company Commanders. We are on very good terms with the infantry and the R.E. who greatly assist us to improve our working dugouts and emplacements.	
			We were kept well informed of the events occurring on the SOMME and elsewhere special wires coming thro' from the Division in addition to the daily intelligence reports of Division Corps and Army.	
			[illegible] Capt.	
			O.C. 120 M.G. Coy.	

2449 Wt. W14957/M90 750,000 1/16 J.B.C. & A. Forms/C.2118/12.

COPIES.

APPENDIX 2

No. 7

COPY No. 1. O.C. 121 M.G. Coy
" " 2. H.Q. 120 Inf Bde.
" 3 S.O. No 1. Section
" 4 " " 2 "
" 5 " " 3 "
" 6 " " 4 "
" 7 WAR DIARY
" 8 FILE.

OPERATION ORDERS. (NO. 5)

BY. CAPT. A. TRAVERS. LACEY
Comdg.
120 M.G. Coy.

RELIEFS The 120 Machine Gun Coy will relieve the 121st M G Coy in the MAROC SECTOR on 12/7/16.

No. 2. Section of 120 M.G. Coy will relieve the following gun ~~teams~~ positions M. 2. 3. 4. & S. 3.

No. 1 " " " " " " R. 9. 10. S. 4. 5

No. 4 " " " " " " R. 14. 15. 16. 17.

No. 3 " " " " " " R. 18. S. 7. 8.

GUIDES One guide from each gun position will be at "~~Hole in the Wall" (MAP REFERENCE. 36c SW. 1/20000 M. 2. d. 4. 8~~) GRENAY CHURCH at 8^4 hours. Gun teams will move off from Billets at 8 minutes interval the first gun team to reach "~~Hole in the Wall~~" GRENAY CHURCH at 8^9 hours. Officers i/c Sections will be at the Iron Gates at 18 hours on 11/7/16 the No. 1s of each gun team to make themselves acquanted with the lines of fire etc.
Their second in Command will proceed with the first gun teams of their respective sections.

HANDING OVER CERTIFICATES When a section has completed its reliefs the S. O. will send at once, an orderly to Coy. H.Qs stating that relief is completed & what stores have been taken over in each Gun position

RELIEF of POINT Z No 1 section will leave behind one guide at Coy. H.Qs to show the two gun teams of 121 M.G. Coy the positions taken over at Point Z (MAP. REFERENCE. 36c SW. 1/20000 M 14. 8. 9½)

TRENCH STORES "B" SERIES The second in Command 120 M.G. Coy will arrange to hand over the stores of the B. Series emplacements to 121. M.G. Coy. as soon as possible after the Relief in the MARCO SECTOR has taken place. The usual handing over Certificates will be rendered.

A Travers Lacey Captain
Comdg 120 Machine Gun Coy

ES.

APPENDIX 3

COPY. NO. 8

No 1. 120th Bde Hqs.
2. 121. M.G. Coy
3. No 1 Sect 120 M.G. Coy
4 2 " "
5 3 " "
6 4 " "
7 File.
8. War Diary.

Operation Orders. No 6.

by. Capt. A. Travers Lacey. Cmdg. 120. M.G. Coy.

RELIEF. The 120th M.G. Coy. will be relieved in the MAROC SECTOR. on Monday. July 12th by the 121st M.G. Coy.

GUIDES. The 120th M.G. Coy will furnish 1 guide per emplacement occupied to report to LIEUT. LOW at GRENAY CHURCH. at 3.50 hours. Four additional men per emplacement will also parade with these guides to help to carry back the M.G. Equipment from the Trenches.

HANDING over CERTIFICATES. Handing over Certificates of all stores will be rendered to the Coy. Hqs immediately a/r relief: these must be signed both by the handing over and the recieving officers.

COMPLETION OF RELIEF. Section commanders will report personally to Coy. Hqs as soon as the relief of their Sections is complete.

PROGRAMME of WORK. Section commanders will hand over to the officers of the relieving Company a statement showing what work has been done and what still requires to be done.

A. Travers Lacey
Capt.

SECRET.

COPIES. 1. 120th Bde.
2. 119 M.G. Coy.
3. 121 M.G. Coy.
4. No 1 Section 120th
5. " 2 " "
6. " 3 " "
7. " 4 " "
8. File
9. War Diary.

Copy No 8

OPERATION ORDER. No. 8.

By. CAPT. A. TRAVERS LACEY. Cmdg. 120 M.G. Coy.

21-7-16

RELIEF. (a) The 120th M.G. Coy will relieve the 119th M.G. Coy. in CALONNE and the guns of 121 M.G. Coy in the Southern subsector of MAROC. on 21-7-16.

(b). Sections will take up the following emplacements:-

No 1. Section	CALONNE	M.G. 6.	S. 5.6.7.
2	"	M.G. 1.	S. 1.2.4.
3 "	MAROC.	M.G. 2.4. S. 3.	R. 10.
4 "	CALONNE.	M.G. C.3.4.	R. 1.9.

(c). One guide per gun will be furnished by 119th & 121. M.G. Coy - they will be at GRENAY ~~Br~~ CHURCH at 17 hours. Teams will move off at 2 minutes intervals. Section officers will proceed with their first guns.

(d). The usual handing over certificates will be rendered: reports that relief is complete will be by telephone thro' Battalions: the code word for "relief complete" being "SAUSAGE".

(e). The two guns in "Z" post will, after relief, move to R.1. and R.9. CALONNE.

A. Travers Lacey, Capt

COPIES
1 - 119 Brig. M.G.C
2 - 120 Inf. Brig.
3 - No 1 Section
4 - No 2 "
5 - No 3 "
6 - No 4 "
7 - War Diary
8 - File

APPENDIX 5.

Copy 7

28/7/16

Operation Orders No 9

By Capt. A. Travers Lacey
Comdg 120 M.G. Coy.

RELIEF. The 120th Brig. M.G.C. will be relieved in the Calonne Sector by the 119th M.G.C at 17 hours on July 29th 1916.

A.

Emplacements to be occupied by relieving Coy. The following positions will be taken over by the four relieving Sections of 119 M.G.C :—

No 1 Section M.G.1 S1. 2. 3
" 2 " S 5. 6. 7 MG.8
" 3 " New Numbers M.G. 15. 17 S10 R21
Old Numbers Maroc MG 2. 4 S3 R10
" 4 " R1. 3. 9 (old number R7) R11 (old number R9)

B.

Guides: One Guide from each of above Emplacements (R3, 11, C3, 4, excepted) will be at Grenay ~~Bridge~~ Church at 16.50 hours.

C

"Z" Post The two gun teams of 120 M.G.C now occupying C3, 4, will relieve the guns of 119 M.G.C from 'Z' post.
This relief to be completed by 16 hours.

D

Carrying Party Five men per gun emplacement (supplied from men now at Coy. H.Q.) will act as carrying parties - They will leave Coy. H.Q. by sections, with five minutes interval between sections, by 16 hours and will report at the respective Section H.Q. in the Trenches. One N.C.O. to be in charge of each section fatigue.

E.

Handing over Certificates The usual handing-over Certificates will be signed & forwarded to Coy. H.Q. on completion of the relief.

F

Completion of Relief. Section Officers will report personally to Coy H.Q. as soon as relief is complete.

G

C3, 4 As the 119 M.G.C. is not taking over ~~positions~~ C3, 4 emplacements O.C. No 4 Section will prepare a duplicate list of the Trench Stores in these emplacements - one copy to be handed over to O.C. 119 M.G.C. for information. The other copy to be forwarded to Coy H.Q.

A. Travers Lacey
Capt.

CONFIDENTIAL

M

2

3

WAR DIARY

OF

120th MACHINE GUN COMPANY

Aug: 1916

A. Travers Lacey
Capt.
O.C. 120. M. G. Coy.

P.1

Instructions regarding War Diaries and Intelligence Summaries are contained in F. S. Regs., Part II. and the Staff Manual respectively. Title Pages will be prepared in manuscript.

WAR DIARY
or
~~INTELLIGENCE SUMMARY~~

(Erase heading not required.)

AUGUST 1916

Army Form C. 2118.

120 Machine Gun Company

Place	Date	Hour	Summary of Events and Information	Remarks and references to Appendices
GRENAY.	1-8-16		Company in billets carries on training. The LOOS SECTOR reconnoitred by Section Officers – all guns of M.G. Coy in this SECTOR are in reserve line except for two which are in support. General impression of emplacements and dugouts is that the latter are good – a lot being in strengthened cellars but the emplacements need a lot of work. The 121st M.G. Coy have started a scheme of work being helped by R.E's: this will be carried on when the Company takes over from them. Weather extremely hot and very little wind. —— · —— A.T.L.	
"	2.8.16		Company training continued – lectures on open fighting and advanced drill. A.T.L.	
"	3.8.16		Operation Orders (No 11) received from 120th Inf. Bde Hqs: the Brigade to relieve 121st Bde in LOOS SECTOR on 4th instant. Infantry and Machine Guns both relieving on same date. Company Operation Orders issued.* In view of fact that LOOS SECTOR was so far from Coy Hqs it was decided not to carry up guns & equipment but take over those of 121st M.G. Coy till night when guns would be taken up to Loos by transport. A.T.L.	*APPENDIX 6
	4.8.16		Company went into LOOS SECTOR. At night one section failed to find Transport with result that guns had to be relieved by fatigue party next morning. This mistake was I consider largely due to fact that a great deal of transport was in Loos owing to infantry reliefs also taking place. In future guns will always be taken up by the teams. Loos was slightly bombarded during the night: Company suffered no casualties. A.T.L.	

P2

Instructions regarding War Diaries and Intelligence Summaries are contained in F. S. Regs., Part II. and the Staff Manual respectively. Title Pages will be prepared in manuscript.

Army Form C. 2118.

WAR DIARY
or
~~INTELLIGENCE SUMMARY~~
(Erase heading not required.)

AUGUST 1916

120 M.G. Coy.

Place	Date	Hour	Summary of Events and Information	Remarks and references to Appendices
GRENAY (Company in trenches in LOOS SECTOR)	5-8-16		Work proposed by 121 M.G. Coy continued – consisting chiefly of making deep dugouts and repairing of emplacements. Quiet day in trenches – little artillery fire on both sides. Excellent weather and a good deal of air work – especially by the enemy, whose aeroplanes are a great deal busier than usual, three or four planes during the day crossing well over our lines. At night our machine guns fired on enemy communications N. of DOUBLE CRASSIER (M.5.c)	A.T.L.
"	6-8-16		Hostile artillery rather active against LOOS VILLAGE and N. end of LOOS CRASSIER, otherwise a quiet day.	A.T.L.
	7-8-16		Enemy's artillery again active against front and support lines all along front of LOOS SECTOR. At night our machine guns opened indirect fire on a suspected headquarters at H.33. A2.10 and on dump at N.1.c.4.4.	A.T.L.
	8-8-16		Hostile artillery not so active but trench mortars more so especially on our support lines N. of DOUBLE CRASSIER. Operation Orders from Brigade received saying that the Division was shortening its front to the former sectors of MAROC and CALONNE – the 16th Div. taking over LOOS on the 9th.	
	9-8-16.		All our machine guns in LOOS relieved by guns of 49th & 47th M.G. Coys. – our machine guns going into MAROC SECTOR: weather very hot and as there were three infantry	

Instructions regarding War Diaries and Intelligence Summaries are contained in F. S. Regs., Part II. and the Staff Manual respectively. Title Pages will be prepared in manuscript.

WAR DIARY
or
~~INTELLIGENCE SUMMARY~~
(Erase heading not required.)

Army Form C. 2118.

Place	Date	Hour	Summary of Events and Information	Remarks and references to Appendices
	9-8-16		brigades concerned with relief at same time the trenches were rather crowded. It would have been better for us if we could have moved from LOOS the day before or after infantry relief. At night our guns carried out indirect fire on communication trenches. A.T.L.	
GRENAY (Coy in trenches in MAROC SECTOR)	10.8.16.		Weather changed. Today is cloudy and have had some rain. Quiet day in trenches - indirect fire by our guns on billets and roads. Operation Orders from 110th Inf Bde, to be relieved by 121 M.G. Coy on 11th. Coy O.O.'s issued* A.T.L.	* Appendix. No 7
	11.8.16		Enemy searched for our machine guns unsuccessfully - we fired during day on billets. Relieved by 121st M.G. Coy in MAROC. 4 guns of Coy sent to CALONNE DEFENCES. 2. Lt. Hardie & party return from M.G. School at CAMIERS. A.T.L.	
GRENAY	12 - 15th 8.16.		This period was occupied to a large extent by making necessary repairs to billets and putting them into as good a condition as possible. A drying room was made - a new Aldershot Oven - wire beds for 60% of the men constructed. Billets were provided with fire buckets and all latrines made to correct pattern - deep - fly proof - with lead rude cover. An extra incinerator was built. Work was also done on two emplacements in the reserve line. The men did physical drill before breakfast and about two hours a day on the guns.	
	15th		LES BREBIS shelled by 5.9 guns: 2 of our mules killed.	

2449 Wt. W14957/M90 750,000 1/16 J.B.C. & A. Forms/C.2118/12.

Instructions regarding War Diaries and Intelligence Summaries are contained in F. S. Regs., Part II. and the Staff Manual respectively. Title Pages will be prepared in manuscript.

WAR DIARY
or
~~INTELLIGENCE SUMMARY~~
(Erase heading not required.)

Army Form C. 2118.

Place	Date	Hour	Summary of Events and Information	Remarks and references to Appendices
GRENAY.	15-8-16		The Company relieved the 119th M.G. Coy in CALONNE SECTOR. The work taken over was chiefly deep dug outs. Permanent fatigues were allotted. Our M.Gs carried out indirect fire. Quiet day in trenches. A.T.L.	* Appendix No. 8.
	16-8-16		Another quiet day - at night our M.Gs fired on roads and billets. Work continued. A.T.L.	
	17.8.16		2. LT. HARDIE att. from 14th H.L.I. sick evacuated. Indirect fire on roads and billets. A.T.L.	
	18.8.16		Another quiet day - indirect fire on communication trenches and roads. The stove pipe attachments are not satisfactory for any prolonged firing - the gas seems to accumulate and when a fresh burst is fired the first shot causes these gases to explode making a big flash and on one occasion splitting the attachment. A.T.L.	
	19.8.16		An internal relief carried out, both officers and men being relieved. Indirect fire carried on. A.T.L.	
	20.8.16 / 21.8.16		Usual indirect fire: on the 21st 2 LT. BRIDGE arrived from Base as reinforcement in place of 2. LT. BARRINGTON killed 29th JULY. A.T.L.	
	22.8.16		On night of 22nd the H.L.I. carried out a raid on the German trenches. In addition to the artillery barrage our M.Gs (six in number) kept up an almost continuous fire on the	

2449 Wt. W14957/M90 750,000 1/16 J.B.C. & A. Forms/C.2118/12.

Army Form C. 2118.

Instructions regarding War Diaries and Intelligence Summaries are contained in F. S. Regs., Part II. and the Staff Manual respectively. Title Pages will be prepared in manuscript.

WAR DIARY
or
~~INTELLIGENCE SUMMARY~~

(Erase heading not required.)

Place	Date	Hour	Summary of Events and Information	Remarks and references to Appendices
			front line of the enemy on the flanks of the portion raided – on communication trenches and reserve line in vicinity. The raid was successful, a wounded prisoner being secured. Our casualties were small. Each of our M.Gs fired about 3,000 rounds and there were only two breakages – muzzle cup and lock spring. A.R.L.	
		23rd	In the evening the A.&S.H. attempted a raid without any artillery or M.G. fire – but wire was too thick. Indirect fire was carried out on enemy billets. A.R.L.	
		24th	The Company should have been relieved today: but at last moment the Division had to take over LOOS SECTOR from the 16th Div. The 119 Bde being in reserve took this SECTOR over. No firing done. 2nd LT HARDIE returns from hospital. A.R.L.	
		25th	Another internal relief. Indirect fire on roads & billets.	
		26th	Informed that 190th Bde were to take over CALONNE SECTOR: our M.G. Coy to be relieved by No 1 Batty M.M. Gs + 5 Hotchkiss guns. O.C. No 1 Batty M.M.G. taken round trenches. Weather bad – the start of ~~[illegible]~~ a great deal of rain. A.R.L.	

2449 Wt. W14957/M90 750,000 1/16 J.B.C. & A. Forms/C.2118/12.

Instructions regarding War Diaries and Intelligence Summaries are contained in F. S. Regs., Part II. and the Staff Manual respectively. Title Pages will be prepared in manuscript.

WAR DIARY
or
~~INTELLIGENCE SUMMARY~~
(Erase heading not required.)

Army Form C. 2118.

Place	Date	Hour	Summary of Events and Information	Remarks and references to Appendices
GRENAY	~~27.7.6~~ 27.6.6		Informed that 111 M.G. Coy was to be attached to 190th Bde & were to relieve us in CALONNE SECTOR on 28th: more rain trenches beginning to be uncomfortable.	
"	~~27.6.16~~ 28.6.16		10.30 AM – 10.40. our artillery carried out a bombardment of enemy trenches opposite CALONNE – little hostile retaliation. O.C. 111 M.G. Coy went round tour of the trenches: more rain – water a foot deep in some trenches.	
"	29 ~~28~~.6.16		111. M.G. Coy relieve us in CALONNE: very bad weather and trenches very sloppy. No casualties during this tour in the trenches.	* appendix No. 9.
"	30 ~~29~~.6.16		Company in billets in GRENAY: day occupied in kit inspection – cleaning guns & equipment and drying mens clothing. more rain.	
	31.6.16.		Weather much better. sections sent for route march of two hours, doing physical drill before breakfast. Work on billets continued.	

[illegible] Capt
O.C. 110 M.G. Coy.

SECRET.

APPENDIX "

COPIES.
No. 1. 120th Inf. Bde.
No. 2. 121. M.G. Coy.
No. 3. No 1 Sect. 120 M.G. Coy
" 4. " 2 "
5. " 3 "
6. " 4 "
7 File
8 War Diary.

Copy No 8.

OPERATION ORDERS. No 10.

By. CAPT. A. TRAVERS LACEY.
Cmdg 120. M.G. Coy.
3-8-16.

RELIEF.

The 120th M.G. Coy will relieve the 121st M.G. Coy in the LOOS SECTOR at 9 hours on August 4th 1916.

(a) GUIDES.

One guide from each emplacement will be at "HOLE IN THE WALL", MAROC at 9 hours. They will be met by the gun teams plus 3 men per emplacement; there will be two minutes interval between arrival of gun teams at "HOLE IN THE WALL".

(b). OCCUPATION OF EMPLACEMENTS.

The distribution of emplacements will be as follows :-

2nd LT. ATTALE. (No 2. Sect.) S.12. S14. R 25. 26. (new numbers)

2nd LT. SCOTT. (No 4 Sect + 3 guns of No 3.). R 27. 28. 29. 30. 31. 32. 33. (")

2nd. LT. FRYER. (No 1 Sect + 1 gun of No 3.) R. 34. 35. 36. 37. 38. 38A. (

(c). CALONNE DEFENCES AND "Z Post".

The four guns in CALONNE and the two guns in Z post will vacate their positions at 6 hours : the positions will be taken over by 121 M.G. Coy as soon as possible after relief in LOOS SECTOR is completed.

(d). Certificates.

The usual handing over certificates will be rendered : on completion of relief Coy. Hqs will be informed by wire - Code word for relief complete will be. MAFISH.

A Travers Lacey Capt.

O.C. 120. M.G. Coy.

COPIES.

No 1 - 121 Brig MGC.
2 - 120 Inf. Brig
3 - No 1 Section
4 - No 2 ..
5 - No 3 ..
6 - No 4 ..
7 - War Diary
8 - File.

APPENDIX. No 7.

9/VIII/16 No 7

Operation Orders No 12

By Capt A. Travers Lacey
Comd. 120 M.G. Coy.

RELIEF

The 120th Brigde M.G. Coy will be relieved in the Maroc Sector by the 121st M.G. Coy at 10 A.M. on Aug. 10th 1916 —

(A) Emplacements to be occupied by the Relieving Coy.

The following positions will be taken over by the four relieving Sections of 121 M.G. Coy. —

Emplacements now occupied by —

No 1 Section.		R 20, 21, S12
2	"	R 25, 26 S11, 14
3	"	R 27, 28, 29 S15
4	"	MG 15, 16, 17 S10

(B) Guides.

One Guide from each Emplacement will be at Grenay Church at 10 A.M.

(C) Carrying Party

Five men per gun emplacement (supplied from men now at Coy. H.Q.) will act as carrying parties. They will leave Coy. H.Q by sections by 9 A.M. and will report at the respective Section H.Q's — one N.C.O. to be in charge of each section fatigue. (Two minutes interval between sections)

(D) Calonne Defences.

At 5 p.m. the 4 guns of No 4 Section manned by one gun team from each Section, under Lieut Parker, will take up positions in Calonne viz:- C1, 2, 3, 4. Four men and one N.C.O. to each gun team [to be detailed by Sectn Comdrs.]

(E) "Z" Post.

From Tomorrow the 10th instant "Z" Post will be occupied by the Company in Calonne — Therefore no guns of 120th M.G. Coy will move to this position on the 10th inst.

(F) Handing-over certificates

The usual handing over certificate will be signed & forwarded to Coy. H.Q. on completion of the relief.

(G.) Completion of Relief

Section Officers will report personally to Coy. H.Q. as soon as their relief is completed.

(Signed)

A Travers Lacey
Capt.

COPIES.

No 1. 120th Inf. Bde
2. 120. M.G.C.
3 No 1 Sect. 120. M.G.C
4 2 " "
5 3 " "
6 4 " "
7 War diary
8 FILE.

APPENDIX No 8

SECRET.
No 7

Operation Orders. No. 13.

by Capt. A. Thomas Lacey Cmdg. 120 M.G.

15-8-16.

RELIEF. The 120. M.G. Coy will relieve the 119th M.G. Coy in the CALONNE SECTOR today 15th Aug. 1916.

GUIDES. Guides of 119 M.G. Coy will be at GRENAY CHURCH at 3.45. P.M. to conduct guntEams to emplacements as follows. (distance of 200x to be maintained between guns.)

No 1. Section (4 guns) to S. 5. 6. 7. and M.G. 8.
" 3 " (4 ") to M.G. 1. S. 1. 2. 3.

CALONNE DEFENSES. The 119. M.G. Coy will relieve the 4 guns of 120 M.G. Coy during the afternoon, in time for relief to be complete by 4. P.M. At 4. P.M. guides of 119 M.G. Coy will be at the CALONNE End of CALONNE SOUTH to guide these four guns to R.1. R.3. R.9. & R. 11.

The OUSELS. 2 guns of No 2 Section will occupy the OUSELS. - no guide will be provided.

CERTIFICATES. Usual handing over certificates will be taken: when relief is complete a report will be sent to Coy Hqs at once. A detailed report of work to be done & no. of men for working parties required will be furnished by Section Officers as soon as possible.

Signed A. Tho. Lacey
Capt

Nos 1: 120 Inf Bgde
" 111 M.G.Coy
3: No 1 Sect. 120 MGC
4: " 2 " "
5: " 3 " "
6: " 4 " "
7: War Diary
8: File.

APPENDIX No 9

Copy No 7

SECRET.

Operation Orders No 14

by Capt. A. Travers Lacey,
Comdg. 120th M.G. Coy.

RELIEF. The 111th M.G. Coy will relieve the 120th M.G. Coy in the CALONNE SECTOR on Aug. 29th inst.

Guides:- Guides from each emplacement and from Sectional Hqrs will be at Grenay Church by 3 p.m. prompt.

No 1's to remain:- The No 1 of each gun team will remain with the relieving Gun Teams until 4 p.m. of the 30th inst. when they will afterwards report independently to the Coy. Hqrs:-

Rations for these No. 1's to be taken up to the trenches by the Carrying Party.

Certificates.- The usual handing-over certificates will be rendered, to be signed both by the Officer taking over and by the Officer handing over

Carrying Party:- A carrying party of 4 men per gun emplacement will be detailed by Section Officers. this party will parade at 2.45 p.m. and will assist the 111th M.G. Coy to take their guns into the trenches and help their own sections out.

Section Officers will report personally to Coy Hqrs on the completion of their relief. They will also give all possible information to the Officer taking over upon the following points:

a) Habits of the enemy.
b) Recent operations of our own & that of the enemy which affects Machine Gunners.
c) The strength, weakness and nature of each emplacement.
d) Targets that have been engaged.
e) Any other information: i.e. Batt. Hqrs, Best methods of visiting guns, usual hours of enemy activity, precautions to be taken - &c.

A. Travers Lacey
Capt
O.C.
120. M.G. COY.

28-7-16

Vol 4

WAR DIARY

OF

120th MACHINE GUN COMPANY.

SEPTEMBER 1916.

A. Travers Leany
Capt.

O.C. 120 M.G. Coy.

SEPTEMBER

Instructions regarding War Diaries and Intelligence Summaries are contained in F. S. Regs., Part II. and the Staff Manual respectively. Title Pages will be prepared in manuscript.

WAR DIARY
or
~~INTELLIGENCE~~ SUMMARY
(Erase heading not required.)

Army Form C. 2118. P1

120 MACHINE GUN COMPANY.

Place	Date	Hour	Summary of Events and Information	Remarks and references to Appendices
GRENAY	1st - 3rd	}	Company in billets in GRENAY. Training included action from limbers and open fighting. A.T.L.	
			(Aug 31st One O.R. sent on cold shoeing course - the establishment provides for 1 cold shoer only which is absolutely insufficient.)	
	3rd		1. Sgt. sent on course to M.G. School CAMIERES A.T.L.	
"	4th		The Company relieved the 121st M.G. Coy in the MAROC SECTOR - sixteen guns in the line. Our trench mortars had been cutting wire for some time and we took over from 121st M.G. Coy the duty of keeping it open during the night. Chief work taken over was the completion of two deep dugouts. The emplacements in this sector are now nearly all provided with deep dugouts. A.T.L.	
	5th		During night of 5th-6th we kept up M.G. fire on wire. A.T.L.	
	6th		Indirect fire on billets and fire on gaps in wire. From about this date there was all along the First Army front a systematic bombardment of enemies front line - particularly on the wire by trench mortars. In case of retaliation our artillery was always to open on to the enemies lines but in the MAROC SECTOR retaliation was rather the exception. Owing to the nature of the ground it was possible for us to lay our M.Gs direct on to gaps cut during the day. We could also fire to observe the effect by day to ensure accurate fire by night. A.T.L.	
	7th		In addition to firing on the wire cross roads - billets & reserve and communication trenches were fired on by our M.Gs. A.T.L.	
	8th		Wire again fired on drawing retaliation from hostile M.Gs: after one of our bursts German	

2449 Wt. W14957/M90 750,000 1/16 J.B.C. & A. Forms/C.2118/12.

Army Form C. 2118.

P2

WAR DIARY
or
INTELLIGENCE SUMMARY
(Erase heading not required.)

Instructions regarding War Diaries and Intelligence Summaries are contained in F. S. Regs., Part II. and the Staff Manual respectively. Title Pages will be prepared in manuscript.

Place	Date	Hour	Summary of Events and Information	Remarks and references to Appendices
GRENAY			Casualties whistles were heard.	
"	9th		At 4 pm in the afternoon we put up a mine in the SOUTHERN CRASSIER. whether our M.G.s opened fire directly after it had gone up. Trench mortar bombardment continues. Enemy transport was heard during the night. our M.G.s searched the roads behind enemy lines	A.T.L
	10th		Indirect fire on roads subsequent on again hearing transport. the Germans now seem to reply to our M.G.s with machine guns. they have also attempted to catch our transport with such fire but considering the noise our transport makes & the obvious route it takes their calculations must be very bad as they never hit it. One dugout completed and new open emplacements dug	A.T.L
	11th		One of our closed emplacements was smashed in by a direct hit from a H.E shell. this emplacement had had other hits & has obviously been spotted – have received permission to relocate it. The sentry was wounded – our first battle casualty. Indirect fire maintained.	A.T.L

2449 Wt. W14957/M90 750,000 1/16 J.B.C. & A. Forms/C.2118/12.

Army Form C. 2118.

WAR DIARY
or
~~INTELLIGENCE SUMMARY~~

(Erase heading not required.)

Instructions regarding War Diaries and Intelligence Summaries are contained in F. S. Regs., Part II. and the Staff Manual respectively. Title Pages will be prepared in manuscript.

Place	Date	Hour	Summary of Events and Information	Remarks and references to Appendices
GRENAY to LES BREBIS	12th		We have moved our headquarters "Billets" from GRENAY to LES BREBIS: unfortunate as we had erected wire beds for 90% of the men - had a good dry canteen - drying rooms etc.: Billets in LES BREBIS not nearly so good but capable of being made good - will start on them at once. ASL	
LES BREBIS	13th		Intermittent fire carried on - also fire on gaps in wire. ASL	
	14th		During the night of the 14th–15th enemy M.G.s were very active - every time they fired we replied with a longer burst - one wonders if our fire is as ineffective as theirs. Trench mortar bombardment continues as does our fire on gaps. ASL	
	15th		Fire as before - Enemy M.G.s again active - two were located. ASL	
	16th		E. Surreys attempted a raid - the cutters were cutting had however made the Hun very alert & they were unable to procure a prisoner. We assisted with five guns sweeping enemies front lines on the flanks - also communication & support trenches. ASL	

2449 Wt. W14957/M90 750,000 1/16 J.B.C. & A. Forms/C.2118/12.

Instructions regarding War Diaries and Intelligence Summaries are contained in F. S. Regs., Part II. and the Staff Manual respectively. Title Pages will be prepared in manuscript.

WAR DIARY
or
~~INTELLIGENCE SUMMARY~~
(Erase heading not required.)

Army Form C. 2118.

Place	Date	Hour	Summary of Events and Information	Remarks and references to Appendices
GRENAY to LES BREBIS	12th		We have moved our headquarters Billets from GRENAY to LES BREBIS: unfortunate as we had erected wire beds for 90% of those - had a good dry canteen - drying rooms etc.: Billets in LES BREBIS not nearly so good but capable of being made good - we start on them at once. A.S.L.	
LES BREBIS	13th		Trench fire carried on - also fire on gaps in wire. A.S.L.	
	14th		During the night of the 14th-15th enemy M.G.s were very active - every time they fired we replied with a longer burst - one wonders if our fire is as ineffective as theirs. Trench mortar bombardment continues as does our fire on gaps. A.S.L.	
	15th		Fire as before - enemy M.G.s again active - two were located. A.S.L.	
	16th		E. Surreys attempt a raid - the continuous wire cutting had however made the Hun very alert & they were unable to procure a prisoner. We assisted with five guns sweeping enemies front lines on the flanks - also communication & support trenches. A.S.L.	

2449 Wt. W14957/M90 750,000 1/16 J.B.C. & A. Forms/C.2118/12.

Instructions regarding War Diaries and Intelligence Summaries are contained in F. S. Regs., Part II. and the Staff Manual respectively. Title Pages will be prepared in manuscript.

WAR DIARY
or
INTELLIGENCE SUMMARY
(Erase heading not required.)

Army Form C. 2118.

P3

Place	Date	Hour	Summary of Events and Information	Remarks and references to Appendices
LES BREBIS.	16th		A Corporal discovered asleep while acting as sentry: was courtmartialled [illegible] reduced to ranks and given 6 months hard labor. Continuous night firing is no doubt a strain on the men the establishment allowance of 1 N.C.O & 4 men per gun cannot meet with the case when a Company is in the trenches with all its guns for 16 days. Unless the Brigade had lent us 100 men it would be absolutely impossible to carry on. A.S.L.	
	17th		Indirect fire continues: we have created a new kind of observation post for sentry. A drain pipe 3" in diameter & about 6' long is put thro the parapet in direction in which gun fires - a sentry post is built round it. The greatest objection to all closed emplacements met so far is that no observation posts were built inside & the sentry can see nothing unless the loophole is opened. A.S.L.	
	18th		We are relieved in MAROC SECTOR by 119 M.G. Coy. Coy in billets in LES BREBIS.	
	19th		Men get a bath - kit inspection & general clean up. Information received that the 120th Bde is to take over 14 BIS SECTOR - (just NORTH of LOOS SECTOR) on 22nd	

Instructions regarding War Diaries and Intelligence Summaries are contained in F. S. Regs., Part II. and the Staff Manual respectively. Title Pages will be prepared in manuscript.

WAR DIARY
or
~~INTELLIGENCE SUMMARY~~
(Erase heading not required.)

Army Form C. 2118.

P4

Place	Date	Hour	Summary of Events and Information	Remarks and references to Appendices
LES BREBIS	20th		14 Bis SECTOR held by 76th Bde - 3rd Division: got into touch with O.C. 76 M.G. Coy & arrange for section officers to reconnoitre line on 21st: on evening of 20th informed that we are to relieve on 21st. A.S.L.	
"	21st		Section officers reconnoitre line early in day. Relief takes place in afternoon. Only 10 guns in the line. 8 in reserve 2 in village line. Dugouts very good – emplacements nearly all open. This I think is the most satisfactory arrangement. This SECTOR is apparently a quiet one – sandwiched in between LOOS & HULLUCH & absolutely in the centre of the LOOS SALIENT. A.S.L.	
LES BREBIS to MAZINGARBE.	23rd		Coy. Hqs Billets moved from LES BREBIS to MAZINGARBE. In 14 Bis SECTOR the German line overlooks ours along the whole front HILL 70 being about in the centre of this sector. We can see little or nothing behind his front line. A.S.L.	
MAZINGARBE	24th		Two extra guns moved up to RESERVE line as a mobile reserve: unusual activity behind German line is reported & his trench mortars & artillery have been very active	

Instructions regarding War Diaries and Intelligence Summaries are contained in F. S. Regs., Part II. and the Staff Manual respectively. Title Pages will be prepared in manuscript.

WAR DIARY
or
INTELLIGENCE SUMMARY
(Erase heading not required.)

Army Form C. 2118.

Ps

Place	Date	Hour	Summary of Events and Information	Remarks and references to Appendices
MAZINGARBE			against HULLUCH sector. Our arty did indirect fire. A barrage scheme ~~with~~ assist artillery was made out - the Salient in German line round PUIT 14 BIS giving us a good opportunity for enfilade fire. A.S.L.	
	25th		We fired on ration dump - light railway & roads behind the German lines. All battle emplacements concealed from ~~air~~ aircraft by having light screens of sandbags & chalk thrown over them. A.S.L.	
	26th		Front line thoroughly reconnoitred with view to possible emplacements for VICKERS guns: I don't think that any will have any better field of fire or put up a better barrage from there than they can from RESERVE LINE. Our M.Gs did indirect fire. A.S.L.	
	27th		News received of fall of THIEPVAL - COMBLES and GUIDECOURT. Another N.C.O. sent on course to M.G. School CAMIERES. A.S.L.	
	28th		Roads & tracks behind German lines were fired on during the night. It is very hard to get any observation in this sector. A.S.L.	

2449 Wt. W14957/M90 750,000 1/16 J.B.C. & A. Forms/C.2118/12.

Instructions regarding War Diaries and Intelligence Summaries are contained in F. S. Regs., Part II. and the Staff Manual respectively. Title Pages will be prepared in manuscript.

WAR DIARY
or
~~INTELLIGENCE~~ SUMMARY

(Erase heading not required.)

Army Form C. 2118.

P6

Place	Date	Hour	Summary of Events and Information	Remarks and references to Appendices
MAZINGARBE	29th		During night of 29th–30th the East Surreys & KORL both entered enemy craters having exploded Bangalore torpedoes. They secured no prisoners as they could find no Germans. A.L. Our arty assisted with covering fire.	
	30th		A new dugout started. Weather is good & should be favourable for operations on the SOMME. ABL.	

2449 Wt. W14957/M90 750,000 1/16 J.B.C. & A. Forms/C.2118/12.

Vol 5

WAR DIARY

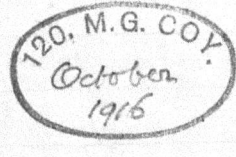

120 MACHINE GUN COMPANY.

OCTOBER 1916

[signature] Major
O.C.
120. M.G. COY:

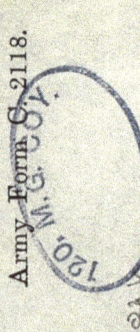

Instructions regarding War Diaries and Intelligence Summaries are contained in F. S. Regs., Part II. and the Staff Manual respectively. Title Pages will be prepared in manuscript.

WAR DIARY
or
~~INTELLIGENCE SUMMARY~~
(Erase heading not required.)

Army Form C. 2118.

120 Machine Gun Company

120. M.G. COY.

Place	Date	Hour	Summary of Events and Information	Remarks and references to Appendices
MAZINGARBE. (Coy. H.qrs) 14 BIS SECTION TRENCHES.	1-10-16		First day in trenches. Work on dugouts carried on. A.R.L.	
	2-10-16 – 4-10-16		In preparation for a minor operation rapid fire by all rifles & M.Gs was carried out at stated intervals during the nights of 2nd 3rd & 4th. On nearly every occasion red lights were sent up by the enemy calling for artillery retaliation although no artillery or infantry action took place on our part. Hostile artillery however retaliated very feebly though his trench mortars were occasionally active. In addition to firing on enemy front line & communication trenches during the stated periods our M.Gs fired on roads & dumps. Average number of rounds fired nightly was about 15,000 - four to five guns being used. Stove pipe attachments as at present issued are no use. They fit so closely that the gas cannot escape with result that gas accumulates & if gun fires for any lengthy period the gas sometimes explodes - on one or two occasions bursting the attachment. A.R.L.	
"	5-10-16		On the night of the 5/6th in conjunction with 8th Division on our NORTHERN flank three gas attacks were launched accompanied by smoke attacks. Enemy fired green rockets & red rockets about four minutes after gas was liberated. After the gas attacks our infantry attempted a raid but were stopped by wire and the very alert state of the enemy. Hostile artillery retaliation was weak. Our M.Gs swept front support reserve & communication trenches. A.J.L.	
"	6-10-16		Quiet day in trenches. Indirect fire on dumps & railways carried on. During the period 1st–6th an advanced Coy. H.qrs was established in the trenches owing to distance from billets. This is the first time it has	

2449 Wt. W14957/M90 750,000 1/16 J.B.C. & A. Forms/C.2118/12.

Instructions regarding War Diaries and Intelligence Summaries are contained in F. S. Regs., Part II. and the Staff Manual respectively. Title Pages will be prepared in manuscript.

WAR DIARY
or
INTELLIGENCE SUMMARY

(Erase heading not required.)

120. M.G. Coy. Army Form C. 2118.

Place	Date	Hour	Summary of Events and Information	Remarks and references to Appendices
6-10-16			been necessary. It brought following points to notice. (a). Four signallers are not sufficient. The Company is supplied with four telephones. In the case of Transport & Q.M.S. stores, advanced headquarters etc. especially when signallers must always be on duty four are quite inadequate. – six seems the minimum. This is specially noticeable if resort must be made to visual signalling by lamp or flags. All officers should go through a short course of MORSE CODE. (b). When guns are fired constantly for long periods during the night the strain on the gun team is great – especially if double sentries are to be posted during hours of darkness. Two cases of sleeping on post have occurred up to date – but in both it seemed evident that the man had been on duty of some kind for very long hours. Single sentries seem sufficient in any line behind the front system. (c). The fact that a company is not provided with a field cooker causes great inconvenience. Each team has to cook for itself – irregularity of meal hours and in some cases danger of location of dugout owing to smoke are the results. (d). Some system must be devised for reading elevating dials at night: a system put into practice by LT. FRYER of No. 1 Section is good. He has had his elevating dials bored at five minute intervals by the R.E. and adjustable pins attached. This prevents errors in reading & also error in elevation due to gradual slipping of elevating wheel.	

2449 Wt. W14957/M90 750,000 1/16 J.B.C. & A. Forms/C.2118/12.

Instructions regarding War Diaries and Intelligence Summaries are contained in F. S. Regs., Part II. and the Staff Manual respectively. Title Pages will be prepared in manuscript.

WAR DIARY
or
~~INTELLIGENCE SUMMARY~~
(Erase heading not required.)

Army Form C. 2118.

120. M.G.

Place	Date	Hour	Summary of Events and Information	Remarks and references to Appendices
MAZINGARBE	6-10-16		(c). With regard to traversing dials – if the zero mark were on the right-hand side of the tripod instead of the left it could easily be read by the No. 2: its present position on the left is very inconvenient. ADL.	
	7-10-16		Very quiet day. In spite of irritation by our artillery especially with trench mortars the enemy retaliation was nil. Indirect fire carried on. ADL.	
	8-10-16		Hostile artillery fairly active: tho' small calibre only. 1 Sgt. sent on Divisional gas course – he returned on 12th having qualified as a gas N.C.O. ADL.	
	9-10-16		Indirect fire as usual.	
	10-10-16		A raid was attempted by the 16th A&S.H. Owing to brilliance of moon enemy had due warning and was not successful. We cooperated by firing on front & support lines. Were informed that Brigade were to move to HULLUCH sector relieving 23rd Bde. Line reconnoitred. Much the same as 14 Bis. 6 guns in RESERVE line – 2 just behind & six in VILLAGE LINE. Dugouts good – only open emplacements in RESERVE line. ADL.	

2449 Wt. W14957/M90 750,000 1/16 J.B.C. & A. Forms/C.2118/12.

Instructions regarding War Diaries and Intelligence Summaries are contained in F. S. Regs., Part II. and the Staff Manual respectively. Title Pages will be prepared in manuscript.

WAR DIARY
or
INTELLIGENCE SUMMARY
(Erase heading not required.)

Army Form C. 2118.

120. M.G. COY.

Place	Date	Hour	Summary of Events and Information	Remarks and references to Appendices
MAZINGARBE to PHILOSOPHE. 14 BIS to HULLUCH Sector.	11-6-16.		Were relieved by 12th M.G. Coy who side stepped from LOOS: relieved 23rd M.G. Coy in HULLUCH. Coy Hqs moved from MAZINGARBE to PHILOSOPHE. Transport & M.S. stores remaining at LES BREBIS. Billets not very good but capable of improvement which was commenced at once. A.S.L.	
	12-6-16		Infantry relief took place. Chief activity within sector is trench mortar. Especially around HULLUCH ~~SG~~ CRATERS. Work taken over was completion of two deep dugouts in RESERVE line. Scheme handed over by 27th Bde for positions of 3 VICKERS GUNS in front line. If proper emplacements can be constructed it will add greatly to security of defence of front line. Indirect fire carried on. From this date targets have been sent in for programme of fire for ensuing 24 hours. This is good as Bde ~~staff~~ leaves it to Infantry who are less inclined to resent constant M.G. fire in consequence of wiring parties & patrols. A.S.L.	
	13-6-16.		Fairly quiet day. N.C.O. sent on clipping course for transport. A.S.L.	

2449 Wt. W14957/M90 750,000 1/16 J.B.C. & A. Forms/C.2118/12.

Instructions regarding War Diaries and Intelligence Summaries are contained in F. S. Regs., Part II. and the Staff Manual respectively. Title Pages will be prepared in manuscript.

WAR DIARY
or
~~INTELLIGENCE SUMMARY~~
(Erase heading not required.)

12.. M.G. COY.

Army Form C. 2118.

Place	Date	Hour	Summary of Events and Information	Remarks and references to Appendices
PHILOSOPHE	14.10.16		Indirect fire carried on as usual.	
TRENCHES IN	15th		1 Officer and 2 O.R. sent on M.G. Course to CAMIERES. Indirect fire carried on.	
HULLUCH SECTION.	16th – 21st		Indirect fire carried on continuously on cross roads, dumps, light railways. Enemy activity confined to trench mortars almost exclusively. Weather bad with much rain. Work carried on with deep dugouts	
	21st		Informed that establishment of M.G. Coy to be increased by 8 gunners per section one driver and one limbered waggon with two draught horses. Arrangements made with Brigade to transfer 33 men from those already attached. Remainder returned to Battalions on 25th. 120th Bde to be relieved shortly by 72nd Bde. Officers of 72. M.G. Coy reconnoitre the line.	
	22nd – 24.		Hostile T.M. very active. Some parts of our line being absolutely destroyed and a good number of casualties inflicted on our troops. The Germans raided the trenches of 121st Bde on our Southern flank.	
	24th		Relieved by 72nd M.G. Coy. Company goes back billets in LES BREBIS.	

Army Form C. 2118.

Instructions regarding War Diaries and Intelligence Summaries are contained in F. S. Regs., Part II. and the Staff Manual respectively. Title Pages will be prepared in manuscript.

WAR DIARY
or
~~INTELLIGENCE~~ SUMMARY
(Erase heading not required.)

Place	Date	Hour	Summary of Events and Information	Remarks and references to Appendices
LES ARERIS.	25–26th		Two days occupied in refitting the Company ready for move.	
to BRUAY	27th		~~Company~~ 120th Inf. Bde move to BRUAY. Need for field cooker again emphasized.	Appendices A. B & C. Bde march time tables
to ORLENCOURT	28th		120th Inf. Bde move from BRUAY to "A" area around ST. POL. Coy in billets in ORLENCOURT. Men in barns. Great difficulty with cooking again. If cooking is not started till new billets are reached by the Company the men have to wait three or four hours for a hot meal. Bad weather emphasizes this.	
to OCOCHE	29th		Bde move to "B" area – Company in billets in OCOCHE. Cooks sent on before loaded with Cook Cart. Weather still bad with frequent rain storms.	
	30–31.		Company in billets in OCOCHE. Advanced Training & tactical schemes. Weather bad.	

ATL

A. [illegible] Major for O.C.
120. M.G. COY.

2449 Wt. W14957/M90 750,000 1/16 J.B.C. & A. Forms/C.2118/12.

SECRET. A. 120. M.G. COY. COPY NO. 5

120TH INFANTRY BRIGADE OPERATION
ORDER NO. 39. 25/10/18.

Ref. Map 1/40,000, Sheet 36B.

1. The 120th Infantry Brigade Group will march to billets in BRUAY on 27th October, as per attached march table.

2. All movements until the junction of the roads at K.34.d.7.1 is reached will be by platoons at not less than 200 yards interval. On arrival at this point the leading platoon of each battalion will halt and the remainder will close up, when the march will be continued as a battalion.

3. First line transport and baggage wagons will march in rear of Battalions.

4. Billeting parties (with bicycles) will meet the Staff Captain at the cross roads at PETIT SAINS (R.2.b.4.7) at 2 p.m. 26th instant.

5. Two lorries have been allotted to each battalion to carry packs and blankets. These lorries will arrive at 8 a.m., and will be loaded under battalion arrangements. Any men left behind to load these lorries will report to Headquarters, 120th Trench Mortar Battery, and will march to BRUAY with that unit, except men left behind by the 13th E. Surr. R., who will join the 120th T. M. Battery at the cross roads at PETIT SAINS (R.2.b.4.7) at 1 p.m.

6. Refilling point for 28th: BRUAY - LABUISSIERE Road.

7. Special orders have been issued to 135th Field Ambulance, who will arrange for a horse ambulance to accompany the Brigade on the march.

8. On arrival in billets, Brigade Headquarters will be established at the HOTEL STREICHET (J.15.b.8.6).

Issued through Signals
at. 8.45 p.m.

H. J. Birrett
Captain,
Brigade Major,
120th Infantry Brigade.

Copy No. 1. 11th R. Lanc. R.
2. 13th E. Surr. R.
3. 14th High. L. I.
4. 14th A. & S. H.
5. 120th M. G. Coy.
6. 120th T. M. B.
7. 120th Signals.
8. B. Bi O.
9. B. Int. O.
10. B. Supply Off.
11. 40th Division "G".
12. 40th Division "Q".
13. 135th Field Amb.
14. No. 3 Co. Div. Train.
15. File.
No. 16. 121st Inf. Bde.
17. 231st F. Co. R.E.
18. A.P.M, 40th Div.
19. File.
20. War Diary.

MARCH TABLE TO ACCOMPANY 120TH
INFANTRY BRIGADE OPERATION ORDER NO. 41.

Unit.	Route.	Destination.	Remarks.
11th R. Lanc. Regt.	ROELLECOURT.	MAISNIL-ST.POL - NEUVILLE AU CORNET.	
14th A. & S. H.	ORLENCOURT.- MARQUAY.- LIGNY.- ST. FLOCHEL.	TERNAS.	To be clear of MONCHY BRETON by 10 a.m.
13th E. Surr. Regt.	BALLEUL AUX CORNAILLES.	AVERDOINGT.	To be clear of BALLEUL AUX CORNAILLES by 10.45 a.m.
14th High. L. I.	MONCHY BRETON.	BAILLEUL AUX CORNAILLES.	Not to enter MONCHY BRETON before 10 a.m.
120th M. G. Coy.	OSTREVILLE - ROELLECOURT.	TACHINCOURT OCOCHE.	Not to pass OSTREVILLE until 11th R. Lanc. R. are clear.
120th T. M. By.	OSTREVILLE.	FOUFFLIN RICAMETZ.	
3 Co. Div. Train.	BAILLEUL AUX CORNAILLES.	LA BELLE EPINE.	not to enter BAILLEUL AUX CORNAILLES before 11.30 a.m.
135th Field Ambuance	To remain at ROCOURT ST. LAURENT.		

C

120. M.G. COY.

SECRET. COPY No. 5.

120TH INFANTRY BRIGADE OPERATION
ORDER NO. 41.

Ref. map 1/100,000 LENS Sheet. 28/10/16.

1. The 120th Infantry Brigade Group will move to billets in area C on 29th October, in accordance with the attached table.

2. Billeting parties will meet the Staff Captain at the cross roads immediately N. of the third E in LA BELLE EPINE, at 7 a.m.

3. The 229th Field Coy. R.E. will join the 120th Infantry Brigade Group on the 30th instant, and will move to billets at AVERDOINGT; march to be arranged by O.C. 229th Field Coy. R.E.

4. The 231st Field Coy. R.E. will remaib at HOUVELIN and will join the 119th Inf. Bde. Group on 1st November.

5. Brigade Headquarters will close at LA THIEULOYE at 10 a.m. and will be established at FOUFFIN-RICAMETZ on arrival in billets.

Issued through
Signals at 6.15 p.m.

[signature] Captain,
Brigade Major,
120th Infantry Brigade.

Copy No. 1. 11th R. Lanc. R.
2. 13th E. Surr. R.
3. 14th High. L. I.
4. 14th A. & S. H.
5. 120th M. G. Coy.
6. 120th T. M. B.
7. 120th Signals.
8. B. B. O.
9. B. Int. C.
10. 40th Division "G".
11. 40th Division "Q".
12. 121st Inf. Bde.
13. 231st Field Co. R.E.
14. 229th Field Co. R.E.
15. 135th Field Amb.
16. Bde. Supply Off.
17. No. ? Coy. D. Train.
18. File.
19. File.
20. War Diary.

MARCH TABLE TO ACCOMPANY 120TH INFANTRY
BRIGADE OPERATION ORDER NO. 40.

Unit.	Starting Point.	Time.	Route.	Destination.	Remarks.
In Order on March: RIGHT COLUMN.					
120th Bde. H. Q. & Sig. Secn.	Cross roads. J.15.c.0.7.	9 a.m.	OURTON - DEVAL - road junction 0.13.c.4.7 - road junction 0.12.d.4.8	LA TRIEULOYE.	
14th High. L. I.	do.	9 a.m.	do.	do.	
11th R. Lanc. R.	do.	9.8 a.m.	OURTON - DEVAL - road junction 0.13.c.4.7 - road junction N.23.b.4.0 road junction N.36. .5.5.	OSTREVILLE.	11th R. Lanc. R. will use the RUE SOUPIRS to get to starting point.
120th M. G. Coy.	do.	9.15 a.m.	do.	ORLENCOURT.	
120 th T. M. B.	do.	9.17 a.m.	do.	do.	
LEFT COLUMN.					
14th A & S. H.	Cross roads J.15.b.5.4.	9.15 a.m.	HOUDAIN - BEUGIN - LA COMTE - HOUVELIN - ROCOURT.	MONCHY-BRETON.	
13th E. Surr. R.	do.	9.23. a.m.	HOUDAIN - BEUGIN - LA COMTE - HOUVELIN	MAGNICOURT-EN-COMTE.	
231st Field Co. R.E.	do.	9.30 a.m.	HOUDAIN - BEUGIN - LA COMTE.	HOUVELIN.	
135th Field Amb. R.A.M.C.	Level crossing - J.15.d.4.1.	9.40 a.m.	HOUDAIN - BEUGIN - LA COMTE - HOUVELIN ROCOURT - MONCHY-BRETON - ORLENCOURT	ROCOURT ST.LAURENT.	
No. 3 Co. Div. Trn.	Will march to HOUVELIN under orders of O.C. No. 3 Coy. 40th Div. Train; head not to pass the level crossing J.15.d.4.1 before 10 a.m.				

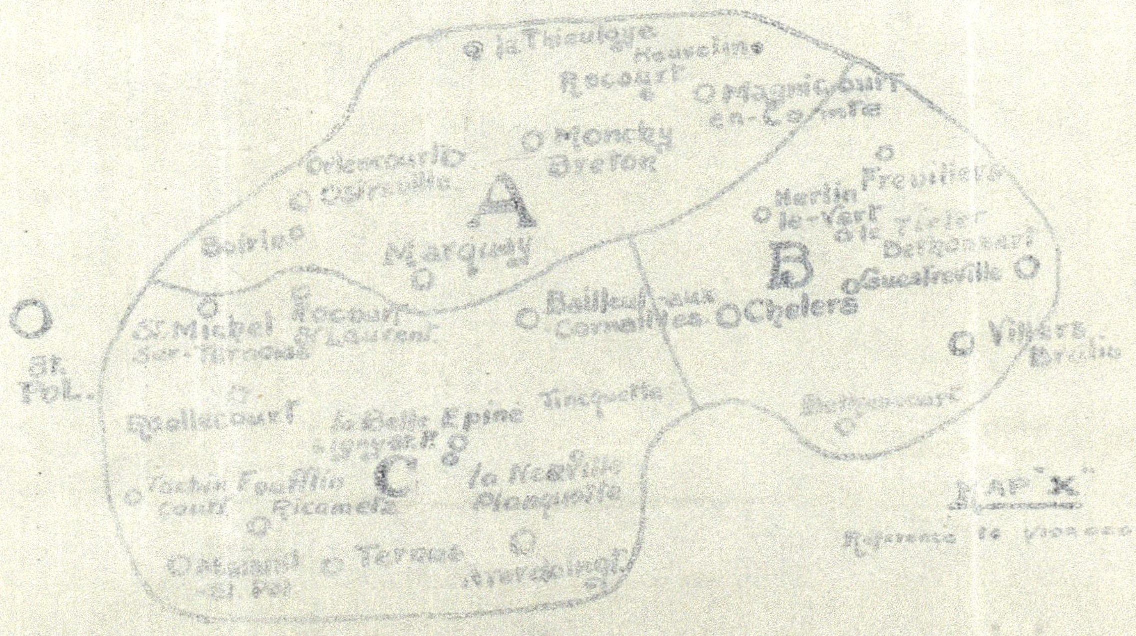

MAP "X"

Reference to [illegible] Map

SECRET. B. COPY NO. 5

120. M.G. COY.

120TH INFANTRY BRIGADE OPERATION ORDER NO. 40. 26/10/16.

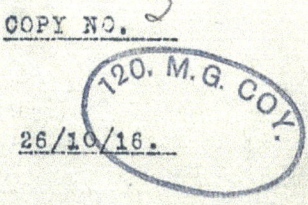

Ref. Map 1/40,000 Sheet 36B.

1. The 120th Infantry Brigade Group will march to billets in Area "A" on 28th October in accordance with attached march table.

2. Billeting parties will meet the Staff Captain at cross roads J.15.b.5.4 at 7 a.m. 28th instant.

3. First line transport and baggage wagons will march in rear of battalions.

4. The 135th Field Ambulance will arrange for one horse ambulance to march in rear of 120th Trench Mortar Battery. This ambulance will be at the starting point for the right column at 9.20 a.m.

5. Lorries will be loaded before marching off, and will proceed to Area "A" under orders from the Staff Captain.

6. Brigade Headquarters will close at BRUAY at 10 a.m. and will be established at LA THIEULOYE on arrival in billets. Reports on the march to the head of the right column.

Issued through Signals at 830 p.m.

H. L. Knott
Captain,
Brigade Major,
120th Infantry Brigade.

Copy No. 1. 11th R. Lanc. R.
2. 13th E. Surr. R.
3. 14th High. L. I.
4. 14th A. & S. H.
5. 120th M. G. Coy.
6. 120th T. M. B.
7. 120th Signals.
8. B. Int. Officer.
9. B. B. O.
10. Bde. Supply O.
11. 40th Division "G".
12. 40th Division "Q".
13. A.P.M., 40th Division.
14. 121st Inf. Bde.
15. 135th Field Ambulance.
16. No. 3 Coy. Div. Train.
17. 231st Field Co. R. E.
18. File.
19. File.
20. War Diary.

No 1000

MARCH TABLE TO ACCOMPANY
120TH INFANTRY BRIGADE
O. O. NO. 39.

Unit.	Starting Point.	Time.	Route.	Destination.	Remarks.
in order of march					
15th E. Surr. R.	Road junction R.2.c.3.7.	8.30 a.m.	HERSIN - BARLIN - RUITZ.	B R U A Y.	Billeting parties will meet units at cross roads in BRUAY (J.16.a.5.7).
14th H. L. Inf.	Road junction L.28.c.2.5.	9.0 a.m.	PETIT SAINS- HERSIN - BARLIN - RUITZ.		
14th A. & S. H.	do.	10 a.m.	do.		
120th B. H. Q. & Signal Section.	do.	10.45 a.m.	do.		
11th R. Lanc. R.	do.	11 a.m.	do.		
231st F. Co. R.E.	do.	12 noon	do.		
120th M. G. Coy.	do.	12.20 p.m.	do.		
120th T. M. B.	do.	12.40 p.m.	do.		

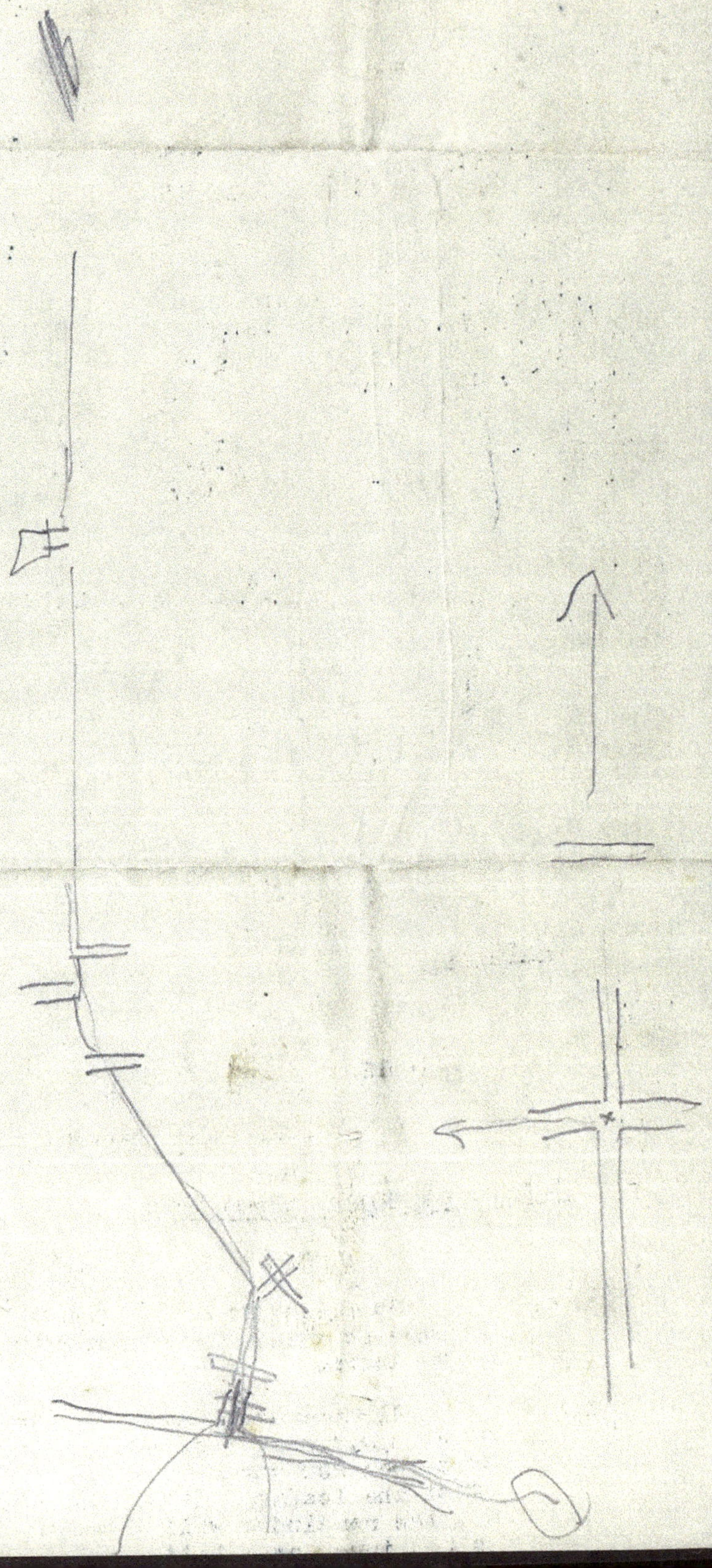

SECRET H 2
120 Inf Bde

SECRET
H 2
120 Inf Bde

Instructions regarding War Diaries and Intelligence Summaries are contained in F. S. Regs., Part II. and the Staff Manual respectively. Title Pages will be prepared in manuscript.

WAR DIARY
or
~~INTELLIGENCE SUMMARY~~
(Erase heading not required.)

Army Form C. 2118.

120 MACHINE GUN COY

Vol 6

Place	Date	Hour	Summary of Events and Information	Remarks and references to Appendices
OCOCHE to SIBIVILLE	1-11-16		Weather still bad. Tactical scheme G.O.C. and staff with commanding Officers and Adjutants of other units in Bde. present.	
	2-11-16 3-4		Bde move to area D – Company in billets in SIBBIVILLE. The following plan was tried here. Immediately on arrival tea was prepared and the men issued with a hot drink. Later on ~~generally~~ about 6 P.M. dinner was served. This is the best method of managing the food question when on the march for units not supplied with a Field Kitchen. We have continued this practice.	Appendices A. B. & C. Bde. March Tables
to NOEUX	4th		Bde move to area J – Company in billets in NOEUX	
to ST. HILAIRE	5th		Bde move to area N – Company in billets in St. HILAIRE	
	6th–10th		Tactical schemes & Drill. Boots & socks wearing out very quick & difficulty found in keeping in touch with D.A.D.O.S.	
	11th		Bde. Tactical scheme in which the Company took part. Information received that the Bde were going into the line.	

2449 Wt. W14957/M90 750,000 1/16 J.B.C. & A. Forms/C.2118/12.

Instructions regarding War Diaries and Intelligence Summaries are contained in F. S. Regs., Part II. and the Staff Manual respectively. Title Pages will be prepared in manuscript.

WAR DIARY
or
~~INTELLIGENCE SUMMARY~~

(Erase heading not required.)

Army Form C. 2118.

120. M.G. COY
November.

Place	Date	Hour	Summary of Events and Information	Remarks and references to Appendices
to DOULLENS	12th		Bde move to billets in DOULLENS and BEAUVAL - Company in billets in DOULLENS. Trenches in HEBUTERNE reconnoitred by C.O. and senior section Officers.	
to BAYENCOURT	13th		Bde. move forward to relieve 148th Inf. Bde. 49th Division - Company in billets in BAYENCOURT. On completion of Relief Bde will come under orders of G.O.C. 31st Division.	Appendices D & E
	14th		Company prepared to relieve 148 M.G. Coy.	Bde March Tables.
to	15th		Right sub-section relieved.	
HEBUTERNE	16th Nov		Left sub. section and guns in reserve relieved. Coy. H.Q. move to HEBUTERNE. Transport & Q.M. Stores remain at BAYENCOURT. In this sector Coy H.Q. in a dugout close up to the line. This was found very convenient. Entrance to splinter proof shelter used by gun team in right subsection blown in & shelter itself rendered useless. No casualties but shelter vacated. Trenches in the whole sector in a very bad state. Indirect fire on roads & billets in GOMMECOURT. Very cold weather.	

2449 Wt. W14957/M90 750,000 1/16 J.B.C. & A. Forms/C.2118/12.

Instructions regarding War Diaries and Intelligence Summaries are contained in F. S. Regs., Part II. and the Staff Manual respectively. Title Pages will be prepared in manuscript.

WAR DIARY
or
~~INTELLIGENCE SUMMARY~~
(Erase heading not required.)

Army Form C. 2118.

120. M.G.C.O. November

Place	Date	Hour	Summary of Events and Information	Remarks and references to Appendices
HEBUTERNE	17/11		Cold and frosty weather. During the night sentries on being relieved fired a few rounds to show that the gun was working. It was found that the cold made the oil very sticky & a series of No 1's was apt to occur till the gun became hot. Glycerine was used in the barrel casing & we had no case of a frozen barrel. Enemy artillery active between 6.30 PM and 8 P.M. against the approaches to the town with the idea of catching our transport. Tear shells were used. No casualties. During the night our M.G.'s fired on roads & billets in GOMMECOURT	~~Appendices D-E~~ ~~Bele Marsh Tables.~~
	18/11		Wet weather and a thaw. Enemy artillery again active against Transport. Several shells fell near Coy. H.2. which is situated near main approach to HEBUTERNE. No casualties.	
	19 Nov		Trenches after yesterday's rain in a very bad state - in several places men were over the knees in mud. Enemy artillery again active in the evening - The artificer ~~being~~ who was stationed at Coy. H.2. being slightly wounded. During the night we again fired on Roads & billets in GOMMECOURT.	

2449 Wt. W14957/M90 750,000 1/16 J.B.C. & A. Forms/C.2118/12.

Instructions regarding War Diaries and Intelligence Summaries are contained in F. S. Regs., Part II. and the Staff Manual respectively. Title Pages will be prepared in manuscript.

WAR DIARY
or
~~INTELLIGENCE~~ SUMMARY
(Erase heading not required.)

Army Form C. 2118.

120. M.G. COY November

Place	Date	Hour	Summary of Events and Information	Remarks and references to Appendices
HEBUTERNE	19/11	(contd)	Information received that the 120 Bde would be relieved by the 92nd & 93rd Inf. Bde. Lt ATTALE proceeded on leave.	
"	20/11		During the day parties of Germans were spotted at a range of 2000 yds. On each occasion they were dispersed by the fire of our guns. 93rd M.G. Coy relieved us in the afternoon in the left subsection and the 92nd M.G. Coy relieved the right subsection in the evening. The Company less Q.M. Stores & Transport which remained at BAYENCOURT spent the night at CHATEAU de la HAIE. No casualties.	Appendices F. G. H & I.
to COIGNEUX	21/11		The Company moves to huts at COIGNEUX. Major Lacey proceeds on leave. LIEUT. T.C. LOW in command of Company.	Bde March Table
to ORVILLE	22 "		The Coy. moves to ~~hut~~ billets in ORVILLE. Very bad roads & several shoes lost on journey. The need for more than one cold shoer badly felt.	
to BERNEUIL	23 "		The Bde move to CANAPLES area - Company in billets at BERNEUIL. No. 24436 L/Cpl. T. Smith sent to Transport Course at ADVANCED HORSE TRANSPORT DEPOT, ABBEVILLE.	
to GORENFLOS	24 "		The Company move to billets in GORENFLOS.	

Army Form C. 2118.

120. M.G. CO.
November

WAR DIARY
~~or~~
~~INTELLIGENCE SUMMARY~~
(Erase heading not required.)

Instructions regarding War Diaries and Intelligence Summaries are contained in F. S. Regs., Part II. and the Staff Manual respectively. Title Pages will be prepared in manuscript.

Place	Date	Hour	Summary of Events and Information	Remarks and references to Appendices
GORENFLOS to ALLIEN	25/11		General clean up of guns and equipment. [initials]	Appendice J March Table.
	26 "		Company move to billets in ALLIEN. [initials]	
	27 " -30 "		Company starts 3 weeks training. First week - Elementary drill and squad drill. Part I Table "C" fired on 30th Nov. [initials]	

[signature] Lt.
for O.C. 120 M.G. Coy

2449 Wt. W14957/M90 750,000 1/16 J.B.C. & A. Forms/C.2118/12.

MARCH TABLE TO ACCOMPANY 120TH
INFANTRY BRIGADE OPERATION ORDER
NO. 43.

Unit.	Starting Point.	Time.	Route.	Destination.
In order of March.				
RIGHT COLUMN.				
Brigade H. Q. & Sig. Sec.	Forked roads ½ mile S. of P. in MAISNIL ST. POL.	9.30 a.m.	Road junction ½ mile N. of A. in MAISNIL ST. POL.- BUNEVILLE - SIBIVILLE - HONVAL	REBREUVE.
14th A. & S. H.	Forked roads ½ mile S. of P. in MAISNIL ST. POL.	9.30 a.m.	BUNEVILLE - SIBIVILLE - Road junction ½ mile N. of Q in SERICOURT.	PT. BOURET and GRAND BOURET.
11th R. Lanc. R.	do.	9.38 a.m.	BUNEVILLE - SIBIVILLE.	SERICOURT.
120th T. M. By.	do.	9.45 a.m.	Road junction ½ mile N. of A. in MAISNIL ST. POL.- BUNEVILLE.	SIBIVILLE.
120th M. G. Coy.	Road junction 200x E. of second E in BUNEVILLE.	10.5 a.m.	BUNEVILLE.	SIBIVILLE.
LEFT COLUMN.				
13th E. Surr. R.	Cross roads N. of V in AVERDOINGT.	9.30 a.m.	GOUY EN TERNOIS - MAGNICOURT SUR CANCHE. - HOUVIN HOUVIGNEUL - CANETTE -MONT - Cross roads ½ mile N. of 1st R. in REBREUVIETTE.	REBREUVE, and LA COUTURE.
14th High. L. I.	do.	9.38 a.m.	GOUY EN TERNOIS - MAGNICOURT SUR CANCHE - HOUVIN HOUVIGNEUL.	CANETTE MONT and HONVAL.
229th F. Co. R.E.	do.	10 am.	As for 13 E. Surr. Regt.	GRAND BOURET.
135th F. Ambulance.	ROELLECOURT CHURCH.	9 a.m.	FOUFFLIN RICAMETZ- TERNAS - BUNEVILLE.	SIBIVILLE.
No. 3 Co. Div. Trn.	Cross roads S. of N in LA BELLEEPINE	9.20 a.m.	TERNAS - BUNEVILLE- MONCHEAUX - HOUVIN HOUVIGNEUL - HONVAL.	REBREUVE.

MARCH TABLE TO ACCOMPANY 120TH
INFANTRY BRIGADE OPERATION ORDER
NO. 44.

Unit.	Starting Point.	Time.	Route.	Destination.	Remarks.
IN ORDER OF MARCH.					
11th R. Lanc. R.	Junction of FREVENT - BONNIERES and FREVENT - BOUQUEMAISON roads ½ mile S.E. of FREVENT Station.	8.13 a.m.	BONNIERES - VILLERS L'HOPITAL.	NOEUX.	Not to halt in FREVENT.
14th A. S. H.	do.	8.21 a.m.	do.	WAVANS and BEAUVOIR.	do.
120th M. G. Coy.	do.	8.29 a.m.	do.	NOEUX.	To be 800[x] behind 11th R. Lanc. R. after passing SERICOURT.
135th F. Ambulance.	do.	8.31 a.m.	do.	VILLERS L'HOPITAL.	
120th T. M. By.	do.	8.36 a.m.	BONNIERES - forked roads ¼ mile E. of last E in CROISETTE.	REMAISNIL.	
No. 3 Co. Div. Trn.	do.	8.38 a.m.	BONNIERES - VILLERS L'HOPITAL - WAVANS.	DRUCAS.	To be clear of REBREUVE by 7.50 am.
13th E. Surr. R.	Cross roads immediately S. of second R in ARBRE.	8.30 a.m.	ARBRE - forked roads S. of E in ARBRES - road junction ¼ mile N. of A in ARBRES - CANTELEUX - C of CANTELEUX - BARLY.	MEZEROLLES	
14th High. L. I.	do.	8.38 a.m.	ARBRE - cross roads ¾ mile S. of D in MON LEBLOND - Cross roads ½ mile S. of first L in MON LEBLOND - MON LEBLOND - BONNIERES.	VILLERS L'HOPITAL.	On Road ARBRE to cross roads N.W. of MON LEBLOND and road from cross roads ½ mile S. of 1st L in LEBLOND to cross roads ¼ mile N. of A in BEAUVOIR impassable.
Bde. H.Q. Sig. Sec.	do.	8.45 a.m.	As for 13th E. Surr. R.	REMAISNIL	B

MARCH TABLE TO ACCOMPANY 120TH INFANTRY BRIGADE OPERATION ORDER NO. 45.

Unit.	Route.	Destination.	Remarks.
Bde. H. Q. Sig. Sec.	HEZEROLLES - LE MEILLARD - BERNAVILLE.	RIBEAUCOURT.	To be South of the river AUTHIE by 9 a.m.
14th A. S. H.	BEAUVOIR RIVIERE - MAIZICOURT - PROUVILLE - BEAUMETZ.	RIBEAUCOURT.	To be South of the river AUTHIE by 8.15 am.
11th R. Lanc. Regt.	BEAUVOIR RIVIERE - MAIZICOURT.	PROUVILLE.	To be South of the river AUTHIE by 8.30 a.m.
120th M. G. Coy.	As ordered by O.C. 120th M.G.Coy.	LE PTOUY. ST. HILAIRE	To be South of the river AUTHIE by 8.45 a.m.
No. 3 Coy. Div. Train.	VAVANS - BEAUVOIR - MAIZICOURT.	PROUVILLE.	To be South of river AUTHIE by 9 a.m.
13th E. Surr. R.	LE MEILLARD - BERNAVILLE.	VACQUERIE and DOMESMONT.	To pass cross roads 1/4 mile N. of S in B. DES FOURNEAUX at 8.15 a.m.
120th T. M. By.	HEZEROLLES - LE MEILLARD - BERNAVILLE.	EPECAMPS.	To pass cross roads 1/4 mile N. of S in B. DES FOURNEAUX at 830 a.m.
[illegible]th Field Ambulance.	FROHEN LE GRAND - FROHEN LE PETIT - LE MEILLARD - BERNAVILLE - DOMESMONT.	LANCHES.	To be South of river AUTHIE by 8.45 a.m.
14th High. L. I.	FROHEN LE GRAND - FROHEN LE PETIT - either H of ST. AUCHEUL-HEUZECOURT - or LE MEILLARD.	BERNAVILLE.	To be South of river AUTHIE by 9 a.m.

NOTE: Units will march independently to their destinations.

10

MARCH TABLE TO ACCOMPANY 120TH
INFANTRY BRIGADE OPERATION
ORDER NO. 48.

Unit.	Route.	Destination.	Remarks.
14th High. L. I.	FIENVILLERS - HARDINVAL - HEM.	DOULLENS.	To pass road junction 300^x N. of first E in BERNAVILLE, at 9 am.
13th E. Surr. R.	do.	do.	To pass above point at 9.15 a.m.
11th R. Lanc. R.	do.	do.	To pass above point at 9.30 a.m.
120th T. M. By.	do.	do.	To pass above point at 9.45 a.m.
120th M. G. Coy.	do.	do.	To pass road junction 200^x N.W. of B in BERNEUIL at 9.45 a.m.
No. 3 Coy. Train.	FIENVILLERS - CANDAS.	BEAUVAL.	To pass road junction 300^x N. of first E in BERNAVILLE at 10 am.
14th A. & S. H.	BEAUVAL.	DOULLENS.	To be clear of BONNEVILLE by 10 am.
12th Yorks Regt.	BONNEVILLE.	BEAUVAL.	Not to enter BONNEVILLE before 10 a.m.

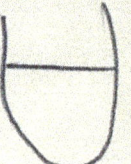

D

PROGRAMME TO ACCOMPANY 120TH INFANTRY
BRIGADE OPERATION ORDER NO. 49.

E

__13th November.__

The 11th R. Lanc. R. and 14th High. L. I. will march to billets in SOUASTRE. Route: MONDICOURT and PAS. Starting point: road junction ¼ mile N. of O in DOULLENS at 9.15 a.m. and 9.30 a.m. respectively. On arrival in billets, 14th High. L. I. will become Brigade Reserve to 148th Inf. Bde.

120th M. G. Coy. and 120th T. M. By. will march to billets in BAYENCOURT. Route: MONDICOURT and PAS. Starting point as for 11th R. Lanc. R., at 9 a.m. and 9.5 a.m. respectively.

12th Yorks Regt. (less 1 company) will march to DOULLENS. Not to enter DOULLENS before 11 a.m.

__14th November.__

11th R. Lanc. R. will relieve 5th York and Lanc. Regt. in Right Subsection. Guides at rate of one for Battalion Headquarters, one per platoon and one per Lewis Gun will be at the road junction K.15.b.0.9 at 10 a.m. Relief to be complete by 2 p.m.

14th High. L. I. will relieve 4th York and Lanc. Regt. in Brigade Support in HEBUTERNE. Guides for Battn. H. Q. and three companies will be at road junction K.15.b.0.9 at 2.30 p.m. Guides for remaining company will be at SOUASTRE Church at 2.30 p.m.

13th E. Surr. R. will march from DOULLENS to billets in SOUASTRE. Route: MONDICOURT and PAS. Starting point: road junction ¼ mile N. of O in DOULLENS, at 9.30 a.m. On arrival in billets 13th E. Surr. R. will become Brigade Reserve to 148th Inf. Bde.

14th A. & S. H. will march from DOULLENS to billets in THIEVRES. Route: AUTHIEULE - ORVILLE. To be clear of DOULLENS by 10 a.m.

12th Yorks Regt. (less one company) will march to billets in BAYENCOURT. Route: MONDICOURT and PAS. Starting point: road junction ¼ mile N. of O in DOULLENS at 9.15 a.m.

One company, 12th Yorks. Regt. will march from BEAUVAL via MARIEUX to VAUCHELLES for work under C. E., XIII Corps.

15th Nov./

15th November.

13th E. Surr. R. will relieve the 4th K. O. Y. L. I. in the Left Subsection. Guides at the rate of one for Battn. H. Q., one per platoon and one per Lewis Gun will be at the road junction K.15.b.0.9 at 10 a.m.

14th A. & S. H. will march to Brigade Reserve in SOUASTRE.
Route: FAMECHON - PAS - HENU. To arrive at SOUASTRE by 12.30 p.m.

½ 120th M. G. Coy. will take over from 148th M. G. Coy. in the Right Subsection. Details between units concerned.

120th T. M. By. will take over from 148th T. M. By. Details between units concerned.

G. O. C. 120th Inf. Bde. will assume command of the section.

16th November.

½ 120th M. G. Coy. will take over from 148th M. G. Coy. in the Left Subsection.

MARCH TABLE TO ACCOMPANY 120TH INFANTRY BRIGADE OPERATION ORDER NO. 54.

Unit.	Route.	Destination.	Remarks.
14th A. & S. H.	N. of river - ORVILLE.	AMPLIER.	To be clear of THIEVRES by 9.30 a.m.
14th High. L. I.	AUTHIE - THIEVRES - N. of river - ORVILLE.	do.	To be clear of AUTHIE by 9.30 a.m.
13th E. Surr. Regt.	do.	do.	To be clear of COUIN by 9.15 a.m.
11th R. Lanc. Regt.	do.	do.	To pass cross roads J.7.b.8.3 at 10 a.m.
120th M.G.Coy.	AUTHIE - THIEVRES- N. of river.	ORVILLE.	To pass cross roads J.7.b.8.3 at 10.30 a.m.
120th T.M.B.	do.	do.	Not to leave COUIN before 10.45 a.m.
No. 3 Co. Train.	N. of river.	do.	To be clear of THIEVRES by 9 a.m.
229th Co. R.E.	-	do.	Not to enter ORVILLE before 2.30 p.m.
135th Field Ambulance.	-	do.	Time and route optional.
224th Co. R.E.	AUTHIE - SARTON - N. bank of river - DOULLENS.	HEM.	To pass cross roads J.7.b.8.3 at 9.30 a.m.
12th Yorks R. (Pioneers). less 1 coy.	AMPLIER.	AUTHIEULE.	To be clear of HALLOY by 9.30 a.m.
1 Coy. 12th Yorks. R.	THIEVRES - N. of river - ORVILLE.	do.	Time optional.

SECRET. COPY NO.

120TH INFANTRY BRIGADE OPERATION ORDER NO. 53.

19/11/16.

Ref. Map. 1/40,000 Sheet 57D.

1. Para. 8 of 120th Inf. Bde. Operation Order No. 52 is cancelled. The 14th A. Suth'd. Highrs. will not move from THIEVRES till further orders are issued.

2. The following moves will take place on 20th November:-

14th High. L. I.	from Brigade Support, HEBUTERNE Section to COIGNEUX, on relief.
12th Yorks Regt (Pioneers).	from BAYENCOURT to HALLOY; to be clear of BAYENCOURT by 9.30 a.m. Route optional.
229th Field Co. R. E.	from BAYENCOURT to HALLOY; to be clear of BAYENCOURT by 9.45 a.m. Route optional.
120th M. G. Co.	From the line HEBUTERNE Section to CHATEAU DE LA HAIE.

3. The following moves will take place on 21st November:-

11th R. Lanc. R.	From Right Subsection to COIGNEUX on relief.
13th E. Surr. R.	From Left Subsection to COUIN on relief.
14th High. L. I.	From COIGNEUX to WARNIMONT WOOD; to be clear of COIGNEUX by 10 a.m.
120th M. G. Coy.	From CHATEAU DE LA HAIE to COIGNEUX; not to enter COIGNEUX before 10 a.m.
120th T. M. B.	From CHATEAU DE LA HAIE and the line to ST. LEGER LES AUTHIE on relief.

4. Billeting parties will report as under at 9 a.m. on the morning of the day on which their respective units move:-

HALLOY ...... to the Town Major's Office.
COIGNEUX .... to the Billet Warden.
COUIN .... to the Town Major's Office.
ST. LEGER.... to the Billet Warden.
WARNIMONT WOOD... to the Town Major, AUTHIE.

5. All movements East of the line SAILLY - COURCELLES to be in bodies not exceeding ½ company, at 200 yards distance.

In the rest of the 5th Army area all movements will be by companies at 200 yards distance, with 500 yards between battalions.

6/.

6. The Right, Centre and Support Company of the 11th R. Lanc. R. are being relieved by the 92nd Inf. Bde. The Left Company of the 11th R. Lanc. R. and the 13th E. Surr. R. are being relieved by the 93rd Inf. Bde.

The G. Os. C. 92nd and 93rd Inf. Bdes. will assume command of their sections as soon as their units have completed the relief of 120th Inf. Bde. Until that time, the G. O. C., 120th Inf. Bde., will be in command of all units in the section.

7. Brigade Headquarters will close at SAILLY AU BOIS on completion of the relief, and will open at the same hour at ST. LEGER LES AUTHIE.

Captain,
Brigade Major,
120th Infantry Brigade.

Issued through Signals
at 11.58 p.m.

Copy No. 1. G. O. C.
2. Brigade Major.
3. Staff Captain.
4. Brigade Signal Section.
5. File.
6. War Diary.
7. 11th R. Lanc. R.
8. 13th E. Surr. R.
9. 14th High. L. I.
10. 14th A. & S. H.
11. 120th M. G. Coy.
12. 120th T. M. B.
13. 12th Yorks Regt. (Pioneers).
14. 224th Field Co. R.E.
15. 229th Field Co. R.E.
16. 181st T. Co. R.E.
17. Left Group, 31st D. A.
18. 94th Inf. Bde.
19. 147th Inf. Bde.
20. 92nd Inf. Bde.
21. 93rd Inf. Bde.
22. 31st Division "G".
23. 31st Division "Q".
24. 40th Division "G".
25. 40th Division "Q".
26. 40th Divn. Train.
27. No. 3 Co. Div. Train.

SECRET. COPY NO. 12

120TH INFANTRY BRIGADE ORDER NO. 57.

25/11/16.

Ref. Maps 1/100,000
Sheets LENS and ABBEVILLE.

1. The 120th M. G. Coy. and 120th T. M. B. will march to billets in AILLIEL and AILLY, and the 135th Field Ambulance will march to billets in FAMECHON on 26th November.

2. Starting point: Road junction ½ mile North of 1st E in ERGNIES, will be passed as under:-

120th M. G. Coy. ... 10.30 a.m.

120th T. M. By. ... 10.40 a.m.

135th Field Ambulance. ... 11 a.m.

3. Units of 121st Inf. Bde. will possibly be marching through AILLY during the morning from FRANCIERES in the direction of VAUCHELLES. Cyclists should be sent on to ensure that the road through AILLY is clear and that these units are not blocked.

4. Billeting parties will report to the Staff Captain at Brigade Headquarters at 8.30 a.m.

5. The billets vacated by the units mentioned in para. 1 will be at the disposal of 14th High. L. I. from 11 a.m.

6. ACKNOWLEDGE.

Captain,
Brigade Major,
120th Infantry Brigade.

Issued through Signals
at 8 p.m.

Copy No. 1. G. O. C.
2. Brigade Major.
3. Staff Captain.
4. Brigade Signals.
5. Brigade Supply Officer.
6. File.
7. War Diary.
8. 11th R. Lanc. R.
9. 13th E. Surr. R.
10. 14th High. L. I.
11. 14th A. S. H.
12. 120th M. G. Coy.
13. 120th T. M. B.
14. 135th Field Ambulance.
15. 229th Field Co. R.E.
16. No. 3 Co. Train.
No. 17. 40th Div. Trn.
18. 40th Div. G.
19. 40th Div. Q.
20. 121st Bde.

14

MARCH TABLE TO ACCOMPANY 120TH INF. BDE. ORDER NO 56.

Unit.	Starting Point.	Time.	Route.	Destination.
120th M. G. Coy.	Road junction 800 yards W.N. of H in ST. HILAIRE.	9.30 a.m.	DOMART - EN - PONTHIEU.	GORENFLOS.
12th Yorks Regt. (Pioneers).	do.	9.55 a.m.	DOMART - EN - PONTHIEU - or FRANQUEVILLE as desired.	AILLY LE HAUT CLOCHER.
14th A. & S. H.	Road junction ½ mile N. of L in MONTRELET	9 a.m.	BERNEUIL - DOMART-EN-PONTHIEU - GORENFLOS - BUSSUS.	YAUCOURT.
229th No. R. E.	do.	9.10 a.m.	do.	YAUCOURT.
13th E. Surr. R.	MONTRELET Church.	9.20 a.m.	BERNEUIL - DOMART-EN-PONTHIEU - GORENFLOS.	BUSSUS.
11th R. Lanc. R.	do.	9.35 a.m.	do.	BUSSUS.
Bde. H. Q. Bde. Signals.	Cross roads ¾ mile S.E. of L in BERNEUIL	10.25 a.m.	BERNEUIL - DOMART-EN-PONTHIEU.	GORENFLOS.
14th High. L. I.	do.	10.30 a.m.	do.	do.
No. 3 Co. Train.	MONTRELET Church.	10.40 a.m.	do.	do.
120th T. M. By.	Cross roads ¾ mile S.E. of L in BERNEUIL	11.5 a.m.	do.	do.
135th Field Amb.	do.	10.45 a.m.	do.	do.

O. C., 135th Field Ambulance, will arrange for one horse ambulance each to follow the 11th R. Lanc. R., 13th E. Surr. R. and 14th High. L. I.

Units will march independently but only the usual hourly halts will be held.

No unit to halt in BERNEUIL or DOMART.

MARCH TABLE TO ACCOMPANY
120TH INFANTRY BRIGADE ORDER NO. 65.

Unit.	Starting point.	Time.	Route.	Destination.
IN ORDER OF MARCH.				
120th M.G.Coy.	Road junction 300 yards S. of A in AUTHIEULE.	9.15 a.m.	AUTHIEULE - N. of river - DOULLENS - forked roads 200 yards W. of LA VOIE DES PRES - JANDAS.	BERNEUIL.
14th High. L. I.	do.	9.25 a.m.	do.	H.Q. and 1 Coy. FIEFFES. 3 Coys. JANAPLES.
229th Co. R.E.	do.	9.40 a.m.	do.	MONTRELET.
135th Field Ambulance.	do.	10 a.m.	do.	FIEFFES.
14th A. S. H.	do.	10.10 a.m.	do.	MONTRELET.
15th E. Surr. R.	do.	10.30 a.m.	do.	BONNEVILLE.
11th R. Lanc. R.	do.	10.45 a.m.	do.	BONNEVILLE.
120th T. M. B.	do.	11.5 a.m.	do.	FIEFFES.
No. 3 Coy. Train.	do.	11.10 a.m.	do.	BONNEVILLE.

Officer Commanding 135th Field Ambulance will detail two horse ambulances to march in rear of 11th R. Lanc. R.

DECEMBER 1916

120 [illegible] Vol. 7

Instructions regarding War Diaries and Intelligence Summaries are contained in F. S. Regs., Part II. and the Staff Manual respectively. Title Pages will be prepared in manuscript.

WAR DIARY

~~or~~

~~INTELLIGENCE SUMMARY~~

(Erase heading not required.)

Army Form C. 2118.

120 Machine Gun Company

Vol 7

Place	Date	Hour	Summary of Events and Information	Remarks and references to Appendices
ALLIEL	1 Dec.		The whole Company put through "Stoppages" on the range. M.L.	
"	2 "		Company inspected by XV Corps M. G. Officer – Lt Col. Clarke. Col CLARKE brought with him & distributed several papers dealing with a new formula to meet every case of "Indirect Fire". M.L.	
	3 "		Tactical scheme arranged by Col. CLARKE, in 5 Officers from each of the M. G. Companies in the Division were present. Chief points dealt with "Control of Guns" and "Combination between M. G. Coys. and LEWIS GUNS". M.L.	
	4 " -7 Dec.		Company carries on with training. Under orders from the Brigade Training was limited to "Elementary Drill & Squad Drill". No tactical work done. M.L.	
	8 Dec.		Major Lacey returns from leave & resumes command of the Company. M.L.	
	9-13th		Owing to the inclemency of the weather training was almost entirely confined to indoor work. On the 11th information was received that the Division were proceeding to the XV Corps middle area around BRAY-SUR-SOMME. Transport to proceed by road and the personnel	

2449 Wt. W14957/M90 750,000 1/16 J.B.C. & A. Forms/C.2118/12.

Instructions regarding War Diaries and Intelligence Summaries are contained in F. S. Regs., Part II. and the Staff Manual respectively. Title Pages will be prepared in manuscript.

WAR DIARY
or
INTELLIGENCE SUMMARY
(Erase heading not required.)

Army Form C. 2118.

Place	Date	Hour	Summary of Events and Information	Remarks and references to Appendices
			by rail.	
	13th		Transport moved off.	
	14th		Company moved from AILLY to MOUFLERS – 6 kilometres.	
	15th		Company moved from MOUFLERS at 6. A.M. and entrained at 7.30 A.M at LONGPRES. detraining at DERNANCOURT at 11. A.M. Marched to Camp 12 on the main BRAY – ALBERT ROAD. In huts built by French: a good deal of mud. Transport arrived at 4. P.M.	
	16th		Clean up and kit inspection etc. Re Transport at M.G. Coy should be provided with a STEWART CLIPPER – have experienced great difficulty in getting horses and mules clipped. 2 pairs of hand clippers cannot cope with 60 animals. A. M.G. Coy has more Transport than an Infantry Battalion with a much smaller personnel and owing to the inadequacy of the gunner personnel extra men cannot be attached to it.	
	16–20th		Most of time spending in cleaning up Camp – making latrines etc. Whole Company put through throwing Mills grenades: old German lines between FRICOURT and MAMETZ visited by entire Company, and a certain amount of useful deductions drawn as regards effect of bombardment on dugouts and emplacements etc.	

2449 Wt. W14957/M90 750,000 1/16 J.B.C. & A. Forms/C.2118/12.

Instructions regarding War Diaries and Intelligence Summaries are contained in F. S. Regs., Part II. and the Staff Manual respectively. Title Pages will be prepared in manuscript.

WAR DIARY
or
INTELLIGENCE SUMMARY
(Erase heading not required.)

Army Form C. 2118.

Place	Date	Hour	Summary of Events and Information	Remarks and references to Appendices
			Percentage of evacuations owing to sickness rather high: chief causes influenza and boils. Every effort made to keep men fit - constant physical exercise: feet rubbed with whale oil daily. News received of French advance at Verdun. (17th)	
	20th		Information received that Brigade was to relieve a brigade of 33rd Div. between RANCOURT and BOUCHAVESNES with the French immediately on the SOUTH.	
	20-22nd		Training confined to huts owing to weather.	
	23rd		O.C. Coy went with Battn Officers to reconnoitre line to be taken over by 120th Bde from 100th Bde. Trenches in very bad condition - greatest drawback being the difficulty of moving men or stores of any kind. Bde HQs in ravine called ASQUITH FLATS about 1 mile S. of LE FOREST. M.G. Coy HQs in another ravine ANDOVER PLACE. 8 guns in line - 4 in front system and 4 in RESERVE SYSTEM. Trench feet very prevalent apparently. Communication trench very bad & practically impassable. Lt. JONES and 2 O.R. proceeded on M.G. Course to CAMIERES	
	26th		Bde relieved 100 Bde. Company had to move off early: it being a 12 mile march men were allowed to ride on limbers as much as possible. Men went in ~~with~~ in fighting order packs & blankets being dumped. Relief started from ANDOVER PLACE at 4.30 P.M.	

2449 Wt. W14957/M90 750,000 1/16 J.B.C. & A. Forms/C.2118/12.

Instructions regarding War Diaries and Intelligence Summaries are contained in F. S. Regs., Part II. and the Staff Manual respectively. Title Pages will be prepared in manuscript.

WAR DIARY
or
INTELLIGENCE SUMMARY

(Erase heading not required.)

Army Form C. 2118.

Place	Date	Hour	Summary of Events and Information	Remarks and references to Appendices
			Completed at 12 P.M.. Two men were stuck in the mud for some hours - one developing trench feet. Enemy must have suspected relief & shelling was much above normal. No casualties going in however. Transport lines - Q.M. Stores & details were back in Ravine about 5 miles away	
	27th		Four guns in front line system can only be reached above ground: guns in Reserve are fairly comfortable. Front line shelled fairly heavily at odd times. It took 5 hours to get rations from ASQUITH FLATS to front line. Solidified alcohol ration very useful. Hot tea sent up every night but it was generally cold before it reached the line	
	28th		Four casualties back at Transport - 1 killed 3 wounded - 2 seriously.	
	29th		Gun teams relieved after 72 hours. So far 4 men sick from front lines 3 cases of trench feet. O.C. 121 M.G. Coy & 1 officer came up to reconnoitre line preparatory to relief on night 31st Dec./1st Jan	
	30th		Trenches worse after a frost - Communication trenches quite impassable. One more case of sickness.	

Instructions regarding War Diaries and Intelligence Summaries are contained in F. S. Regs., Part II. and the Staff Manual respectively. Title Pages will be prepared in manuscript.

WAR DIARY
or
INTELLIGENCE SUMMARY

(Erase heading not required.)

Army Form C. 2118.

Place	Date	Hour	Summary of Events and Information	Remarks and references to Appendices
	31st		Another casualty – 1 man in front line seriously wounded in stomach. Relieved at night by 121 M.G. Coy. The relief was sent by motor bus from MAUREPAS to CAMP 17 at SUZANNE. Total casualties sick 8 – battle casualties 1 killed 4 wounded.	
			This is the first experience of the SOMME the Company has had and they have done well. It seems absurd to have VICKERS GUNS in front line trenches when dugouts do not exist – in some cases tripods could not be taken up.	
			[illegible] Major O.C. [illegible] M.G. Coy 31-12-16.	

2449 Wt. W14957/M90 750,000 1/16 J.B.C. & A. Forms/C.2118/12.

CONFIDENTIAL.

Vol 8

WAR DIARY

of

120th MACHINE GUN COMPANY

VOLUME 8 January 1917

[illegible] Major

O.C. 120 M.G. Coy.

Vol 8

War Diary

Army Form C. 2118.

Place.	Date.	Hour.	Summary of Events and Information.	Remarks and references to appendices.
SUZANNE.	1-1-17		Company at CAMP 17 near SUZANNE having been relieved from BOUCHAVESNES NORTH SECTOR on night 31st Dec. 1916. Day spent in cleaning clothes - kit inspection etc. O.C. saw M.G. Corps Officer and discussed plan of M.G. defence in sector just left. Weather good. A.T.L.	
"	2-1-17		Physical exercise: party detailed to make roads under orders from CAMP COMMANDANT. Men given a New Year tea and concert in the evening. Orders from Brigade that the Brigade will relieve the 119th Bde in RANCOURT SECTOR on the 4th inst. A.T.L.	
"	3-1-17		2nd in C. and two section officers go to RANCOURT SECTOR to reconnoitre and make arrangements for relief of 119 M.G. Coy. A.T.L.	
" RANCOURT.	4-1-17		Coy leaves CAMP 17 at 12 midday by motor buses to MAUREPAS - march from MAUREPAS to RANCOURT via COMBLES. Relief of 119 M.G. Coy complete by 8 P.M. 4 guns in Support - no dugouts or emplacements - in very exposed positions which could only be visited by night. 4 guns in RESERVE with fairly good shelters and all on reverse slope of hill defiladed from view of enemy. A.T.L.	
	5-1-17.		Application made to Bde for R.Es to work on dugouts - especially S. positions. Day quiet on the whole. A.T.L.	
	6-1-17		Went round positions with the Corps M.G. Officer: discussed advisability of traverse in a night line scheme also the probable effectiveness of reverse of bands of fire which deduct (a) all cross in front of front line or (b) in front of reserve line. S positions relieved. A.T.L.	
	7-1-17		In the evening work was commenced on three deep dugouts for "S" positions - work can only go on during hours of darkness. A.T.L.	

War Diary.

Army Form C. 2118.

Place.	Date.	Hour.	Summary of Events and Information.	Remarks and references to appendices.
RANCOURT.	8-1-17		Inter-section relief: work continued on dugouts - weather cold.	
	9th		Two anti aircraft emplacements built and manned by Section in Support. Very cold and a light fall of snow in the early morning. Importance of camouflage in construction of dugouts & concealment of tracks very much impressed by the snow.	
"	10th		Inter section relief. Weather better but very cold. Progress with dugouts fairly good.	
	11th		Transport officer Lt. BROOMAN had an accident being rolled on by his horse - finally evacuated to England. Rather active day for artillery but we had no casualties - enemy aircraft busy particularly between 3 and 4 P.M.	
SOZANNE	12th		Relieved in RANCOURT SECTOR by ~~HQ~~ 121 M.G. Coy. No casualties during this Tour. Company was sent back in buses from MAUREPAS to CAMP. 17. near SUZANNE.	
	13		Cleaning up guns & equipment: heavy snow fall during the night	
	13-17.		Company at CAMP. 17. resting. No training except physical drill & indoor work was possible on account of the weather - Snow on the ground during the whole of the period.	
	18.		Relieved the 119 M.G. Coy in the BOUCHAVESNES NORTH SECTOR which had been greatly improved since our last visit - the continuous cold weather had made the ground very hard & all mud had disappeared. Only five guns in position when we took over. 1 in support 4 in reserve. All positions being worked on by a Tunnelling Coy.	
	19		Weather still hard and dry. Snow showed up tracks very distinctly	

WAR DIARY.

PLACE	Date	Hour	Summary of Events and Information.	Remarks & references to appendices
BOUCHAVESNES NORTH	19th		Two more guns put into line - into Corps M.G. positions - deep dugout but no emplacement. Two guns doing anti aircraft work. Light very good and enemy machines very active. Enemy artillery fired 300 gas shells into ravine in which Coy HQs and many dugouts were situated: respirators were put on. A slight wind kept the fumes from settling but respirators were worn for nearly two hours. Gas was apparently K gas. No casualties	
	20th		Work continued on five emplacements and dugouts - also two more guns put in position in CORPS LINE. Anti aircraft dugout being built by R.E. our anti aircraft guns were busy. Frosty weather continues. Enemy artillery not so active as during last tour in this ~~[illegible]~~ Sector - probably because trenches were better & less movement located.	
	21st		More aerial activity: I do not consider that Machine Guns have much chance of bringing down aeroplanes with the present contrivances sights - understand that new ones are being brought out.	
	22nd		Inter Sectional relief. Usual aeroplane activity. frost continues.	
	23.		~~As~~ Hun aeroplane brought down. Claims submitted by Anti air craft guns and our machine guns. Apparently it was brought down by a French aviator in a S.P.A.D. aeroplane. Lt. LOW proceeds to ENGLAND on special leave on compassionate grounds. Lt FRYER takes over 2nd in command. A reinforcement officer arrives. Lt SHARPE and takes over duties as	

ARMY FORM. C2118

WAR DIARY.

PLACE	Date	Hour	Summary of Events and Information	Remarks & references to appendices
BOUCHAVESNES NORTH.	24–26th		Work continued on dugouts – weather still frosty on some days as many as 23° of frost being registered. Aircraft busy & the enemy machine being brought down. O.C. 24 M.G. Coy reconnoitres the line. OAL.	
	26th		Relieved by 24. M.G. Coy. Company taken in buses to CAMP 12 four miles W. of BRAY. No casualties during this tour in the trenches. OAL.	
CORBIE	27th		Coy. marched to billets in CORBIE.	
	28–31st		Most of this time was spent cleaning up transport, limbers and equipment. Men were given plenty of physical exercise etc. OAL.	
	30th		O.C. 1 officer & 2 N.C.Os attend a lecture on aircraft and a new sight for M.Gs when engaging hostile aircraft. This should be good but has not had any testing yet. OAL.	

[illegible]
Major

125th M.G. Coy
VOL 9

Instructions regarding War Diaries and Intelligence Summaries are contained in F. S. Regs., Part II. and the Staff Manual respectively. Title pages will be prepared in manuscript.

WAR DIARY
or
~~INTELLIGENCE SUMMARY.~~
(Erase heading not required.)

Army Form C. 2118.

120 MACHINE GUN COMPANY

Vol 9

Place	Date	Hour	Summary of Events and Information	Remarks and references to Appendices
CORBIE	1-2-17		Company in billets at CORBIE. Weather fine but very cold 23° of frost being registered on two or three occasions. Training consisted chiefly of gun work in the morning and the system of Recreational Training in the afternoon i.e. football running boxing etc. etc.	
	2-2-17		Four officers attended a demonstration at flying ground with idea of recognizing our own aircraft and getting ideas of heights and speeds for anti aircraft work with machine guns: on questioning pilots it appeared that M.Gs seldom bother aircraft if at a height of more than 2000 ft. At elevation of 1500 ft an ~~[illegible]~~ aeroplane should be engaged successfully by M.Gs. etc.	
	3rd-10th		Usual training carried on. O.C. Coy visited at the 6th Corps H.Qs. Officers of XV & III Corps to inspect two anti aircraft mountings. The Lewis rifle mounting seems the better.	
	10th		2 officers and 4 O.R. attached to A.A battery for a week to learn to recognize our own and hostile planes, judge elevations etc. No M.G. work was done.	
			Company moved from billets in CORBIE to CAMP 111 1 mile N of BRAY.	
	11th		Moved from Camp 111 to CAMP 112 in same locality. Horses under shelter. Frost still holding and weather good	
	11-14th		Training carried on and work done on harness and limbers.	
	15th		O.C. ordered to visit 8th Div. Hqs. The Coy is to be attached to 8th Division for an operation which is to take place at end of February in the BOUCHAVISNES SECTOR	

A5834 Wt. W4973/M687 750,000 8/16 D. D. & L. Ltd. Forms/C.2118/13.

Confidential/702.

Vol 10

WAR DIARY
of
120th MACHINE GUN COMPANY.

VOL. 10.

Feb. 16th - March 31st 1917.

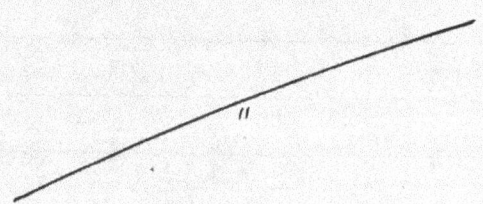

VOL. No 10.

Army Form C. 2118.

WAR DIARY
or
~~INTELLIGENCE~~ SUMMARY.

(Erase heading not required.)

Instructions regarding War Diaries and Intelligence Summaries are contained in F. S. Regs., Part II. and the Staff Manual respectively. Title pages will be prepared in manuscript.

FEB. 16 1917 – MARCH. 31. 1917

120. Machine Gun Company.

Place	Date	Hour	Summary of Events and Information	Remarks and references to Appendices
CAMP 112.	16		O.C. reconnoitred ground in RANCOURT SECTOR to decide on position of guns etc. Task allotted to Company was to put up a barrage on the N. flank of attack. Positions of groups of guns settled – exact position of one gun in each group settled and table showing location of gun, target, clearances etc. submitted to CORPS. M.G. officer.	
	18.		Conference at 8th Bde. Hqs. Points re Signals – stores – rate of fire etc. settled.	
	16–22.		All gun kit overhauled – depression stops fitted to certain guns – and new night firing boxes made.	
RANCOURT SECTOR.	23rd		Coy moved into trenches at RANCOURT.	
	24.		Exact position of each gun settled and work commenced on emplacements – shelters and section dumps	
	25th		Work continued – 1 casualty – 1 O.R. wounded	
	26th		Emplacements etc almost complete – operations which were to have been on 27th postponed to 28th	
	27th		Operations postponed to 2 or 3. MARCH	
	27–3rd		Extra cover put on shelters. M.G. barrage slightly altered giving greater clearances vertically & horizontally. 1 officer reinforcement arrives. (2 LT BENNETT) LT LOW struck off strength (medical board) 28th. LT FRYER. 2nd in command to date 1-3-17	
	3rd		Orders received at 5 P.M. that attack was to take place at 5.15. A.M. on 4th. Guns in position and all ready by 7. P.M. 1 officer (2 LT SCOTT slightly wounded but at duty) 1. O.R. killed	
	4th		Infantry attacked at 5.15. M.G. barrage from 5.21 to 5.31. Rate of fire 125 rounds per minute. Average rounds per gun 1100	

Instructions regarding War Diaries and Intelligence Summaries are contained in F. S. Regs., Part II. and the Staff Manual respectively. Title pages will be prepared in manuscript.

WAR DIARY
or
~~INTELLIGENCE SUMMARY~~.
(Erase heading not required.)

Army Form C. 2118.

Place	Date	Hour	Summary of Events and Information	Remarks and references to Appendices
RANCOURT SECTOR.	4th		During night of 4-5th intermittent fire from guns on barrage lines to prevent enemy massing for counter attack. AH	
	5th		Relieved from barrage positions by 23rd M.G. Coy. Total casualties during operations Officers slightly wounded 1 O.R. killed 4 O.R. wounded. (A detailed account of operations including all orders dispositions maps etc submitted to CORPS M.G. officer later.) AH	
CAMP 21 SUZANNE			Company moves to CAMP 21 ½ near SUZANNE. Company ceases to be attached to 9th Division	
	6th		Information received that 125th Inf Bde to move to BETHUNE ROAD SECTOR and relieve 98th Inf Bde on 7th. O.C. reconnoitres line and arranges details of relief. 2 Lt. HARDIE goes sick. AH	
BETHUNE ROAD SECTOR.	7th		Coy relieves 98 M.G. Coy in BETHUNE ROAD SECTOR - all sixteen guns in line. Six on CORPS LINE - 4 in support 2 in close support and four in front line. Only four officers available in addition to C.O. 2nd in Command and transport officer. AH	
	8th		Recommended that two of the guns in the front line be moved back to unoccupied Corps positions - this was done. Quiet day with only a few light shells - rifle grenades etc on front line. AH	
	9th		Very quiet day - heavy artillery fire heard from direction of South of SOMME. Suspect that enemy may be preparing to retire from his positions in front of us. AH	
	10th		Another suspiciously quiet 24 hours - work continued on dugouts etc and SAA & Very lights carried up. AH	

A5834 Wt. W4973/M687 750,000 8/16 D. D. & L. Ltd. Forms/C.2118/13.

Instructions regarding War Diaries and Intelligence Summaries are contained in F. S. Regs., Part II. and the Staff Manual respectively. Title pages will be prepared in manuscript.

WAR DIARY
or
INTELLIGENCE SUMMARY.
(Erase heading not required.)

Army Form C. 2118.

Place	Date	Hour	Summary of Events and Information	Remarks and references to Appendices
BETHUNE ROAD CENTRE	10th		From this date hostile artillery activity renewed – a number of shells being blind and apparently coming from a long distance. Reconnoitred bty positions with view to rearrangement of the defence scheme.	
	11th		Hostile artillery active – chiefly on two points (a). Vicinity of BETHUNE ROAD and ridge by ROAD Wood. News of enemy retirement further NORTH coming through – active patrolling done and apparently enemy line in front of us still fairly strongly held.	
	12.		Artillery active again on same localities. Scheme for readjustment of guns submitted and approved by Brigade	
	13.		Enemy active with artillery, grenades, rifles & bullets, continued news of German retreat and fires seen behind German lines. 2/LT SCOTT who had been slightly wounded on 3rd is sent to hospital. Only 3 officers apart from O.C. i/c Command now available for trench duty.	
	14		Usual activity. Inter section reliefs.	
	15		Hostile artillery & aircraft very active. 2/LT PARKER goes to hospital with ulcered foot – LT FRYER sent on M.G. Course to CAMIERES also 2 N.C.Os. Have now only two officers on duty in the trenches to look after 16 guns.	

Instructions regarding War Diaries and Intelligence Summaries are contained in F. S. Regs., Part II. and the Staff Manual respectively. Title pages will be prepared in manuscript.

WAR DIARY
or
INTELLIGENCE SUMMARY.
(Erase heading not required.)

Army Form C. 2118.

Place	Date	Hour	Summary of Events and Information	Remarks and references to Appendices
BETHUNE ROAD SECTOR.	16.		Hostile shelling much below normal. Orders received from Brigade re advance in case of enemy withdrawal.* This entailed attaching two M.G.s to each front line battalion. 2/Lt Page, reinforcement, reports for duty.	Orders attached 120th Bde No. 81
	17		Raid to be carried out ~~tonight~~: raid cancelled on receipt of news that the Germans had probably evacuated his lines. Orders received that the Bde was to move forward on morning of the 18th. All	
	18.		German lines entered without any opposition: positions as laid down in 120 Bde. O. 81. taken up. Line reconnoitred and guns disposed of as follows. Four guns in main line of defence 4 in close support, four in support and four in reserve.* No signs of enemy though patrols pushed forward. All.	*. List of positions as sent to Bde on 18th.
	19th		~~[struck through]~~ Corps mounted troops ordered out. Main line of resistance of Bde moved forward to line HILL 150 - HAUT ALLAINES - COPSE WOOD. Four guns from reserve moved into this line. Orders received that 120th Bde Bde relieved by 119th Bde. All	
	20th		Relieved by 119 Bde M.G. Coy - handed over everything except guns & spare parts. Company moved back to huts near CURLU. Casualties during this tour - NIL. All	
	21st		Clean up equipment guns etc. All	
	22nd		~~[struck through]~~ Men had baths - whole Brigade moves up nearer line. Company in dugouts near HEM WOOD.	

A5834 Wt. W4973/M687 750,000 8/16 D. D. & L. Ltd. Forms/C.2118/13.

Instructions regarding War Diaries and Intelligence Summaries are contained in F. S. Regs., Part II. and the Staff Manual respectively. Title pages will be prepared in manuscript.

WAR DIARY
or
INTELLIGENCE SUMMARY.
(Erase heading not required.)

Army Form C. 2118.

Place	Date	Hour	Summary of Events and Information	Remarks and references to Appendices
~~[illegible]~~ HERMWOOD LOCALITY	23.		Whole brigade at work on roads. Orders received that 65th Div. was to be relieved by advance of XI CORPS – relief to be complete by noon 25th. Bde not affected by this. Another officer reinforcement 2/Lt ROBKIN in place of Lt HARDIE evacuated sick to England. all.	
	24–28–31		Company doing road work and training. Staff rides under G.O.C. 125th Inf Bde. all.	
			Atkinson Lacey Major O.C. 125 M.G. Coy	

Headquarters
120th Inf Bde.

17-3-17

Distribution of Machine guns and fields of fire as follows.

2 guns at C. 26. d. 9. 2. firing (1) 1. 3 central
(2) C. 27 d. 5. 5

2 guns at C. 27 b. 5. 5. firing (1) C. 22. d. 5. 0
(2) C 28. c. 3. 0.

2 guns in local support at C 21 d. 7. 6.
2 " " " " LACEY REDOUBT
(C. 20 d. 8. 8.)

4 guns in RESERVE in MORGAN TRENCH
4 guns in " in ROAD WOOD

Coy. Headquarters still at ROAD WOOD.

A Travers Lacey
Major

O.C. 120 M.G. Coy

SECRET. COPY NO. 5

120TH INFANTRY BRIGADE ORDER NO. 81.

Ref. 1/10,000 BOUCHAVESNES.
1/20,000 62 c. N.W.

15th March, 1917.

1. (a) In case of a voluntary withdrawal by the enemy on the front of XV Corps, touch is to be maintained and all trenches vacated by him are to be occupied.

(b) Large forces are not to be committed to TORTILLE VALLEY until the high ground to the West side of the valley has been made good.

(c) As soon as the line - spur running S.S.E. in C.26.d. and I.2.b. (on which stands MAJDAN SUPPORT trench) - thence approximately the line of the MERMAN trench - BROUSSE trench - SINOPE trench - ANGORA trench - GERMAIN WOOD trench - HILL trench - is firmly in our hands, covering parties will be pushed forward to seize the passages over the TORTILLE and the Canal du Nord.

(d) When this line has been occupied, a further advance to the heights East of the valley will be initiated.

(e) In case of hostile counter attack by superior forces, our present front line is to remain the main position for defence.

2. The boundary between the 40th Division and 8th Division will be - C.15.d.6. - junction of BROUSSE ALLEY and BROUSSE trench - C.22.c.9.9 - COPSE ALLEY - all inclusive to the 8th Division.

3. The Divisional Commander intends to carry out the role allotted by a gradual forward movement, in echelon, of the Left and Centre - The movement to be in close touch with, and initiative taken from, the 8th Division.

4. The dividing line between Brigades will be - present point of junction in Front line to Main road at C.26.d.3.5. to TORTILLE river about I.X.c.5.0 (i.e. ALLAINES inclusive to left brigade).

5. In case of voluntary withdrawal of the enemy, the 120th Infantry Brigade, in conjunction with the advance of the 25th Inf. Bde. on its left, and taking the initiative from them, will occupy the successive steps in echelon from N. to S. DETVA trench, DETVA support, and BROUSSE trench. On the right of our front the advance will be made by steps to MERMAN trench, and such part of MERMAID as is necessary to cover the right flank, touch being maintained with Brigade on our right.

6. The Battalion in Left Subsector (13th E. Surr. R.), taking the initiative from the Brigade on its left, will move forward to the line C.22.c.9.9. exclusive - C.27.b.30.05 exclusive.

7. The Battalion in Centre Subsector (14th High. L. I.), will move forward to the line C.27.b.30.05 inclusive to C.26.d.6.5.

8. The Battalion in Left Subsector will be the directing battalion.

9. The Reserve Battalion (14th Arg. & Suth'd. Highrs.) will move to OLD QUARRY and support the left battalion.

10. The Right Battalion, (11th R. Lanc. R.), will remain in its present position, supporting Centre Battalion (14th High. L. I.).

11. O. C., 120th M. G. Co., will place two guns each at the disposal of Left Battalion (13th E. Surr. R.) and Centre Battalion (14th High. L. I.).

12. O. C., 120th T. M. B., will move his reserve guns to MADAME.

13. Brigade Headquarters will be established at MADAME.

14. O. C., 231st Field Co. R.E., will place one section at the disposal of the O. C., Left Battalion (13th E. Surr. R.) and O. C., Centre Battalion (14th High. L. I.).
H. Q. and 2 companies will remain at P. C. VIOLETTE and await orders.

15. O. C., Left Group, 40th D. A., will arrange for protective barrages in accordance with these moves.

16. The new positions will be consolidated after which covering parties, in the form of strong patrols, will be pushed out along whole front to discover and seize the crossings over the Canal du Nord and TORTILLE river.
Reports on crossings to be forwarded as early as possible to Brigade Headquarters - especially as regards those which carry the roads

Main BETHUNE Road.
BOUCHAVESNES - ALLAINES.

(R.E. reconnaissance should accompany those patrols to report on bridges and roads).

17. All units moving forward will carry flares for communicating position to aircraft. Special precautions to be taken to guard against land mines or other traps left by the enemy.

18. ACKNOWLEDGE.

Smfairns

Lieutenant,
a/Brigade Major,
120th Infantry Brigade.

Issued through Signals
at / p.m.

Copy No. 1.	11th R. Lanc. R.	No. 9.	119th Inf. Bde.
2.	13th E. Surr. R.	10.	121st Inf. Bde.
3.	14th High. L. I.	11.	25th Inf. Bde.
4.	14th A. & S. H.	12.	40th Div. "G".
5.	120th M. G. Co.	13.	40th Div Art (Left Group).
6.	120th T. M. B.	14.	File.
7.	231st Field Co. R.E.	15.	File.
8.	13th Yorks Regt.	16.	War Diary.

A

VOLUME 11

Instructions regarding War Diaries and Intelligence Summaries are contained in F. S. Regs., Part II. and the Staff Manual respectively. Title pages will be prepared in manuscript.

120. M.G. COY
APRIL 1917

WAR DIARY
or
INTELLIGENCE SUMMARY.
(Erase heading not required.)

Army Form C. 2118.

Vol XI

120th MACHINE GUN COY.

Place	Date	Hour	Summary of Events and Information	Remarks and references to Appendices
DUG-OUTS near HEM WOOD (MAP. REF. 62. C.N.W. 1:20,000. H.3.C.)	1st APRIL. 1917.		Company in rest: 40th Division out of the line. Weather very changeable but mild. 2Lt. C.J. ROWLAND returns to Company after being absent sick since Dec. 1916. 2 N.C.OS go on 3 days course to Div. Gas School. all Transport inspected by O.C. 40th Div. Train. + A.D.V.S.	
	2nd		Company continues advanced training with idea of breaking away from usual trench warfare routine and encouraging initiative amongst the men. 120th Bde hold a Staff ride attended by O.C. Coy and 1 other officer - principles of advance and rear guard actions discussed on ground. Information received that XV CORPS line of resistance is now roughly SAULCOURT - GUYENCOURT - SOREL - FINS - YTRES. 40th Div. to be prepared to occupy old line of resistance - LIERAMONT - NURLU - EQUANCOURT. Reconnaissance arranged re positions - distribution of troops - approaches etc. 119th & 121st Bde to take up above line in case of necessity. 120th Bde to be in reserve. G.O.C. 120th Bde holds conference at 6.30. P.M. Routes - state of roads etc. discussed. all	
	3rd	9.30 a.m.	O.C. Coy and 2nd in C. reconnoitre on horseback roads in above area. On the whole good.	
		9.30 P.M.	Orders received from Brigade re routes - places of assembly etc. Weather better - high wind - our aeroplanes active. all	[redacted]
	4th		Heavy snow nearly all day: orders received that 40th Div. was to take over centre area of XV CORPS front from 8th & 20th Divisions on 6th inst. 121st Bde to be in the line 119th in Div reserve at MANANCOURT and ETRICOURT: the 120th Bde to be in CORPS RESERVE and not move at present. 2 N.C.OS return from Gas School both qualified - one distinguished.	[redacted]
	5th		Four officers sent to reconnoitre area as above. Visit from Corps. M.G. Officer and discussion re difficulties of communication and mutual support in open warfare. Tactical scheme suggested at which G.O.C. Brigade and battalion Commanders are to be present. Weather very fine - our aeroplanes active by day and night. 1. O.R. sent on leave to U.K. U.S.A. in state of war with Germany. Allies within 2 miles of St QUENTIN.	

A5834 Wt. W4973/M687 750,000 8/16 D. D. & L. Ltd. Forms/C.2118/13.

Instructions regarding War Diaries and Intelligence Summaries are contained in F. S. Regs., Part II. and the Staff Manual respectively. Title pages will be prepared in manuscript.

WAR DIARY
or
~~INTELLIGENCE SUMMARY.~~
(Erase heading not required.)

Army Form C. 2118.

Place	Date	Hour	Summary of Events and Information	Remarks and references to Appendices
DUGOUTS NR HEM. WOOD.	6th APRIL.		Training carried on: report on inspection of transport on 1st received - entirely satisfactory. Weather very unsettled - with two or three sharp showers. AH	
	7th		A tactical scheme was carried out by one section: weather very unsettled. Official news received of declaration of war by U.S.A. on Germany. AH	
	8th		Church services - weather excellent. AH	
	9th		News received that the Third Army had attacked and taken all objectives - one Corps taking 2,000 prisoners: news unofficial but forwarded through Division & Brigade. Weather bad again - showers of hail & rain. Route march in the afternoon. Later report states that 1st, 3rd & 5th Armies had attained all objectives - prisoners taken between 6000 - 7000. Later report states that whole of Vimy RIDGE & FARBUS captured: our troops have reached POINT DE JOUR and FEUCHY CHAPELLE-DE-FEUCHY and NANCOURT - all 3rd objectives: prisoners estimated at 7000. Cavalry ordered forward. This appears to have turned the N. flank of the HINDENBURG LINE. AH	
	10th		Working party supplied to load lorries etc. from 7.30 - 10 A.M. Weather very wet again. Report received that on the north the enemy had counterattacked but been repulsed everywhere - prisoners now 8000	
	11th		Tactical Scheme at which G.O.C. Bde. Corps M.G. Officer & 2 Coy Commanders were present: chief lesson rapid reconnaissance of ground and necessity for Infantry Commanders to cooperate when Sections were allotted to Battalions. Lt. FRYER & 4 O.R. return from course at CAMIERS: Lt. SCOTT reports from hospital.	

A5834 Wt. W4973/M687 750,000 8/16 D. D. & L. Ltd. Forms/C.2118/13.

Instructions regarding War Diaries and Intelligence Summaries are contained in F. S. Regs., Part II. and the Staff Manual respectively. Title pages will be prepared in manuscript.

120. M.G. COY.

WAR DIARY
or
~~INTELLIGENCE SUMMARY.~~

(Erase heading not required.)

Army Form C. 2118.

Place	Date	Hour	Summary of Events and Information	Remarks and references to Appendices
Nr HEM WOOD.	11th		Report received re operations near ARRAS. MONCHY LE PREUX occupied: Hindenburg Line broken opposite RIENCOURT-LES GAGNICOURT & HENDECOURT-L.G. by V Army who are advancing: total captures :- 11000 prisoners and 103 guns. 163 M.Gs & 60 T.M.S. Weather cold - fall of snow in the evening.	
	12th		Orders received that Company was to move to EQUANCOURT to prepare billets for Brigade.	
EQUANCOURT.	13th		Company moved to EQUANCOURT. Village much damaged by the enemy during retirement. All work on billets:	
	14th		Orders received that 10 guns were to be lent to 121st Bde in view of an attack which they were to make shortly on the villages of BEAUCAMP & VILLERS PLOUICH. These guns to be in reserve positions: line reconnoitred. Consisted of strong points only - system practically that of outposts in advance with ~~[illegible]~~ open fighting.	
	15th		Ten guns moved into line and two put on A.A. work near METZ-EN-COUTURE. Weather wet again.	
	16th		Bde HQs & 2 battns move into EQUANCOURT. Orders received that 121st Bde are in line & to be relieved by 120th & 119 Bde. on 17th inst. line reconnoitred. 1 O.R. sent on leave to U.K.	
	17th		Relieved 121st M.G. Coy. All positions on reverse slopes - limbers taken up to gun positions for relief. 12 guns in line.	
	18th		Orders that 40th Division would shortly attack in conjunction with 8th Div. on S. flank & 20th Div. on N. flank. 1st objectives for 120th Bde enemy outpost trenches - 2nd objectives for Bde. villages of BEAUCAMP & VILLERS PLOUICH. LIEUT. SCOTT sent down sick.	
	19th		Weather better & line fairly quiet.	
	20th		8th Div. took GONNELIEU. 2 guns attached to 11th K.O.R.L.	

A5834 Wt. W4973/M687 750,000 8/16 D. D. & L. Ltd. Forms/C.2118/13.

Army Form C. 2118.

Instructions regarding War Diaries and Intelligence Summaries are contained in F. S. Regs., Part II. and the Staff Manual respectively. Title pages will be prepared in manuscript.

WAR DIARY
or
~~INTELLIGENCE SUMMARY.~~
(*Erase heading not required.*)

Place	Date	Hour	Summary of Events and Information	Remarks and references to Appendices
EQUANCOURT	21st		11th K.O.R.L. on N. flank take objectives: enemy outpost trenches, & capture 2 M.G.'s & on S. flank 13th E.S. take enemy outpost trenches. Total prisoners between 50 & 60. 2 guns moved up in to close support on S. flank.	
	22nd		Patrols of left Batt^n capture 2 prisoners. Find BEAUCAMP strongly held. Artillery cut wire in front of & shell BEAUCAMP. Co^y H^d qrs move to DESSARTWOOD.	
	23rd		Orders received that Div^n will assault villages of VILLERS PLUICH & BEAUCAMP & gain footing on heights beyond.	
			2 guns moved up to outpost line to fire (1) BOAR COPSE - BILHEM (2) S. of BEAUCAMP to high ground N. of VILLERS.	
			2 guns moved to outpost line to fire from high ground N. of VILLERS to BOAR COPSE.	
			2 " . . . . R.1.d. central to R.8.a central.	
			2 " . . . . R.8.a.3.7. - R.8.2.9.8.	
			8 " in reserve at Gouzeaucourt WOOD.	
			During night 23/4 artillery active against objectives.	
	24th	4.15am.	14 A. & S.H. on N. attack BEAUCAMP, get through village but are driven back & entrench in old GERMAN trench W. of village. 13 E.S. attack & take VILLERSPLUICH & heights beyond. Total prisoners: 1 unwounded officer, 3 wounded officers; 314 unwounded & 16 wounded O.R. also 3 M.G.'s. 2 O.R.'s of Co^y slightly wounded by H.E.	
	25th	4.16	14 A. & S.H. relieved by 11 K.O.R.L. who take BEAUCAMP & consolidate line 300 yds E. of village. Enemy heavy artillery shell METZ.	
	26th		BEAUCAMP & VILLERSPLUICH shelled throughout the day. Otherwise a quiet day. Co^y relieved by 121 M.G. Co^y. Returned to billets in EQUANCOURT. 1 N.C.O. sent on leave to U.K.	
	27th		8 guns moved up to second reserve line & 2 put on AA work in EQUANCOURT.	
	28th		Major LACEY left for course at CAMIERS. Tested captured M.G. on Range.	
	29th		Church parades. Baths for 35 men. Orders received that Co^y w^d relieve 121 M.G. Co^y on 1/2 May.	
	30th		Relief arranged with 121 M.G. Co^y. Co^y held athletic sports.	

[signature]

A5834 Wt. W4973/M687 750,000 8/16 D. D. & L. Ltd. Forms/C.2118/13.

Confidential.

Vol 12

WAR DIARY

of

120 MACHINE GUN COMPANY

Volume 12 : MAY 1917

[illegible] Major

O.C. 120 M.G. Coy

31-5-17

VOLUME 12

MAY 1917

Instructions regarding War Diaries and Intelligence Summaries are contained in F. S. Regs., Part II. and the Staff Manual respectively. Title pages will be prepared in manuscript.

WAR DIARY
or
~~INTELLIGENCE SUMMARY.~~
(Erase heading not required.)

Army Form C. 2118.

120th MACHINE GUN Coy.

Place	Date	Hour	Summary of Events and Information	Remarks and references to Appendices
DESSART WOOD 57c S.E. 1/20.000 W1a.9.2	MAY 1st	8pm	120 Machine Gun Coy relieved 8 Guns of 121 M.G. Coy in VILLERS-PLOUICH and BEAUCAMP Sector. 119 M.G. Coy relieve 4 of our Guns from BROWN LINE in GOUZEAUCOURT AREA. 4 guns remain in position in BROWNLINE round GOUZEAUCOURT WOOD. Our artillery heavily shelled LA VACQUERIE during day & night. Hostile artillery shelled VILLERS PLOUICH & BEAUCAMP during the night. 8 new gun positions constructed in the new intermediate line running behind VILLERS & BEAUCAMP. 1 N.C.O returned from leave in U.K. 1 reinforcement reported from Base. 1 N.C.O. sent to C.C.S with accidently self-inflicted wound. R.S.G.	
	2nd		4th Guards Machine Gun Coy. Officers were shown round all gun positions with a view to taking them over. LT SCOTT returned from C.C.S. Weather fine. Our artillery shelled LA VACQUERIE intermittently during the day. Hostile artillery retalliated on VILLERS & BEAUCAMP. Considerable aerial activity both hostile & own. Village of HAURINCOURT reported burning. R.S.G.	
	3rd	10am	Our four guns in BROWN LINE at GOUZEAUCOURT WOOD were relieved by 4th Guards M.G. Coy. These guns remained in reserve in GOUZEAUCOURT WOOD. Received orders that 120 M.G. Coy would be attached to 121 Brigade for operations about to take place in the immediate future. 1 officer reinforcement (2/LT MACFARLANE) reported from Base. Hostile artillery fairly inactive. Own artillery registering during the day. LA VACQUERIE shelled intermittently. Considerable aerial activity. R.S.G.	
	4th	8.30am	8 Guns in intermediate line relieved by 4th Guards M.G. Coy. Section officers reconnoitre & fix barrage positions in 121 Brigades area for operations to be carried out the following night. Barrage scheme arranged cooperating with 119th, 121st Brigades & 2nd Division under the Corps Machine Gun Officer.	

A7092). Wt. W128 9/M1297 750,000. 1/17. D. D & L., Ltd. Forms/C2118/14.

Instructions regarding War Diaries and Intelligence Summaries are contained in F. S. Regs., Part II. and the Staff Manual respectively. Title pages will be prepared in manuscript.

VOLUME 12

WAR DIARY
or
INTELLIGENCE SUMMARY.
(Erase heading not required.)

Army Form C. 2118.

120th MACHINE GUN COY

Place	Date	Hour	Summary of Events and Information	Remarks and references to Appendices
DESSART WOOD	4th contd	-2.15am	Our artillery carried out a practise barrage on LAVACQUERIE at 4.50am, during the day cut wire & carried out destructive shoots in LAVACQUERIE area. Very considerable aerial activity. Enemy barraged our front line from 4.7am – 4.45am in answer to our barrage. R.S.F.	
	5th	11pm –3.15am	A Raid on LAVACQUERIE and SONNET FARM position was carried out in cooperation with the 8th Division. The moon was near the full but the sky being overcast, the night was dark. 120 Machine Gun Coy had 16 guns in position & put down a barrage cooperating with 119th and 121st Brigade & 8th Div. Machine Gun Coys. The enemy put down a defensive barrage but this seemed to be in patches. Casualties in this Company 1 O.R. killed. During the raid a searchlight was active from HINDENBURG LINE N of LAVACQUERIE R.S.F.	
	6th	3.15am	All 16 Guns withdrawn from barrage positions & kept in Reserve in Gouzeaucourt Wood.	
		3.3pm	Relieved 4th Guards Machine Gun Coy in old positions in intermediate line. 3 O.R. casualties. 1 killed. 2 wounded. LAVACQUERIE reported burning in the morning and a huge fire seen in SONNET FARM. A good deal of aerial activity. 5 hostile planes over our lines. Wire (Intelligence) In the BULLECOURT Sector, our troops still hold 1300 yards of the front & support trenches in the HINDENBURG LINE, E of the village in spite of counterattacks. 900 prisoners captured by us since night 2/3rd May on the front LOOS – BULLECOURT. Lt ROWLAND proceeded to U.K. on leave. C.S.M. returned from 1 months leave in U.K. R.S.F.	
	7th		Reconnoitred with Corps M.G. officer & C.R.E. the new BROWN LINE which runs through Q35d.5.2. & Q20.b.5.5. sited 6 new gun positions in 120th Brigade Sector. Several hostile observation balloons up during the day. A few enemy aeroplanes observed flying high. Artillery activity normal. R.S.F.	

A7092). Wt. W1289/M1297 750,000. 1/17. D. D & L., Ltd. Forms/C2118/14.

Instructions regarding War Diaries and Intelligence Summaries are contained in F. S. Regs., Part II. and the Staff Manual respectively. Title pages will be prepared in manuscript.

VOLUME =/12

MAY 1917.

WAR DIARY
or
INTELLIGENCE SUMMARY.
(Erase heading not required.)

Army Form C. 2118.

120th MACHINE GUN COY.

Place	Date	Hour	Summary of Events and Information	Remarks and references to Appendices
DESSART WOOD	MAY 8th		Weather Changed, Rained hard all day, Exceedingly quiet all along the front. 6 new M.G. emplacements constructed & occupied in BROWN LINE R.S.F.	
	9th		Weather fine. Artillery normal. About 12 noon 12 Enemy aeroplanes flew high over our lines, in an encounter between an enemy machine one of our machines was brought down & landed between DESSART WOOD & METZ en COUTURE Considerable movement seen in the HINDENBURG LINE. We have established sniping posts about 400x in front of our line to deal with the above movement. R.S.F.	
	10th		2 OR reported from BASE as reinforcements. Our Artillery carried out registration during the day. Hostile Artillery below normal. VILLERS PLOUICH. BEAUCAMP & INTERMEDIATE LINE shelled about 10.30 am 11.30 am & 4 pm. no damage done. R.S.F.	
	11th		Weather continues fine. O.C. 60 M.G. Coy reconnoiters our Gun positions & arranges to relieve guns in intermediate line next day. Enemy reported working on his wire & repairing his trenches. Own & hostile aeroplanes active during the day many hostile observation balloons up during the day. Hostile aeroplane came down apparently out of control as it took a nose dive from a considerable height Our Artillery fired on parties of the Enemy & in retaliation to enemy bombardment of BEAUCAMP & VILLERS R.S.F.	
	12th	8 pm	60 Machine Gun Coy relieved our Guns in intermediate line & 20th Div M.G. Coy relieve our Guns in Brown line. 1 Section of 4 guns sent to SOREL LE GRAND & HEUDECOURT to relieve No 24 M.G. Coy's A.A. Machine Guns.	
HEUDECOURT		11 pm	120 Machine Gun Coy move into HEUDECOURT & become part of Reserve Brigade to 8th Division. Orders to man the BROWN LINE of GONNELIEU SECTOR with 16 Guns in case of S.O.S. Orders received cautioning all ranks against loitering in the SQUARE of HEUDECOURT as this is believed to be mined. R.S.F. L/Cpl Stewart proceed to U.K. to join a CADET SCHOOL.	

A7092). Wt. W128.9/M1297 750,000. 1/17. D. D & L., Ltd. Forms/C2118/14.

VOLUME III/12.

WAR DIARY
or
~~INTELLIGENCE~~ SUMMARY.
(Erase heading not required.)

Army Form C. 2118.

Instructions regarding War Diaries and Intelligence Summaries are contained in F. S. Regs., Part II. and the Staff Manual respectively. Title pages will be prepared in manuscript.

MAY 1917

120th MACHINE GUN COY.

Place	Date	Hour	Summary of Events and Information	Remarks and references to Appendices
Ref 57c.S.E. W.12.b.6.9.	13th		120th Machine Gun Coy relieved 23rd M.G. Coy in the GONNELIEU SECTOR having 6 guns in the front line & 6 in the Intermediate line keeping 4 guns back in reserve at Coy Hd Qrs. posting 2 guns on A.A. work. 9 O.R. reported from Base as reinforcements. During relief the enemy made a small raid on our front line, rifle & M.G. fire was opened on the raiding party who immediately dispersed leaving 2 wounded prisoners in our hands. Our casualties nil. R.S.L.	
	14th	3.am	Violent Thunderstorm, unusually heavy rain causing much inconvenience. Hostile & own Artillery quiet. Considerable aircraft activity. R.S.L.	
	15th		Decided to re-distribute front line guns, withdrawing two back to intermediate line, making this line much more strongly held with M.G.'s. Artillery Activity normal. Aerial activity Nil. Enemy active with aerial darts & T.M.'s on our front line. R.S.L.	
	16th		Raining hard, slightly misty. Fairly quiet along front. C.Q.M.S. returned from 10 days leave in U.K. Pte Boyce proceeded on leave to U.K. Corpl (A/Sergt) Pearce ~~[illegible]~~ tried by Field General Court Martial for accidently negligently wounding himself with a Revolver. Orders received to reconnoiter the BROWN LINE (3rd System) 4 Reserve guns to occupy positions in case of S.O.S.	
	17th		Weather slightly better. Artillery fairly active. Enemy shelling our front line with Gas Shells. Aerial activity nil. Lt ATTALE & 2 O.R. proceed to join M.G. Course at CAMIERS. 7 O.R. reported from Base as reinforcements. R.S.L.	

A7092). Wt. W12839/M1293 750,000. 1/17. D. D & L., Ltd. Forms/C2118/14.

Instructions regarding War Diaries and Intelligence Summaries are contained in F. S. Regs., Part II. and the Staff Manual respectively. Title pages will be prepared in manuscript.

VOLUME III/12.

MAY 1917.

WAR DIARY
or
~~INTELLIGENCE SUMMARY.~~

(Erase heading not required.)

Army Form C. 2118.

120th MACHINE GUN COY.

Place	Date	Hour	Summary of Events and Information	Remarks and references to Appendices
W.12.b.6.9.	18.		Weather fine. Enemy artillery more active than usual. Own aircraft active. Hostile aircraft nil. 2nd/Lt. ROSKIN sent down wounded. Notice received that 1 O.R. evacuated on 10.5.17. RGS	
	19.		Proficiency Pay - Class II - granted to 3 O.R. - one of whom No 46638 - Pte BEECHAM. J. was evacuated on 17.2.17. One O.R. returned to duty. Work - making shelters at W.12.b.6.9. Aerial activity normal. One BRITISH machine brought down in flames by hostile machine near GOUZEACOURT VILLAGE at about 4.30 p.m. RGS	
	20.		O.C. and 2 O.R. return from M.G. course at CAMIERS. Weather excellent - good deal of aerial activity. One O.R. proceeds on leave to U.K. One O.R. returned to duty. Two O.R. evacuated. Artillery activity normal. Enemy shelled EAST side of GONNALIEU VILLAGE from about 5 to 5.30 p.m. RGS	
	21.		Transport inspected by A.D.V.S. and O.C. Dn. Train - good report. Continued aerial activity. Artillery activity normal. One O.R. admitted to hospital. RGS	
	23		2nd/Lt. NORMAN and 3 O.R. reported as reinforcements to Coy. Weather fine. Artillery & aerial activity normal. RGS	
	24		One O.R. proceeds on leave to U.K. One O.R. admitted to hospital. Great aerial activity. Hostile artillery shelled GONNELIEU - EASTERN side of Village, & also WESTERN edge of VILLERS GUISLAIN. RGS	

A7092). Wt. W12839/M1293 750,000. 1/17. D. D & L., Ltd. Forms/C2118/14.

Instructions regarding War Diaries and Intelligence Summaries are contained in F. S. Regs., Part II. and the Staff Manual respectively. Title pages will be prepared in manuscript.

VOLUME ~~III~~ 12

WAR DIARY
or
~~INTELLIGENCE SUMMARY.~~

(Erase heading not required.)

Army Form C. 2118.

MAY. 1917. 120th MACHINE GUN COY.

Place	Date	Hour	Summary of Events and Information	Remarks and references to Appendices
W.12.b.6.9.	25.		2nd LIEUT. THOMPSON reports as reinforcement. Two O.R. admitted to Hospital. The 104th M.G. Coy relieved five guns on the right - 2 in front line and 3 in the intermediate line. The 104th Inf. Brigade take over the right ~~[illegible]~~ half of the GONNELIEU SECTOR. Weather fine. RBS O.C. (Major A.T. LACEY) mentioned in SIR D. HAIG'S dispatches. Supplement to London Gazette 25:5:17. RBS	
	26.		120th Inf Bde took over from 119th Inf Bde right half of latter's sector. The 120th Inf. Bde's front now extends from R.27.d.3.4 to approx. R.14.d.0.1. Seven M.G. positions taken over - three in or near front line + 4 in intermediate line. Gas trench mortar shells put over by enemy on our front line NORTH-EAST of GONNELIEU. ~~Lieut FRYER proceeds on leave to U.K.~~ RBS One O.R. wounded. One O.R. admitted to hospital. A great deal of aerial activity by both ourselves + enemy. One enemy machine fires M.G. at our front line NORTH-EAST of GONNELIEU - one of our machines + the enemy machine brought down about R.26.d.2.1. Weather fine. RBS	
	27.		Weather fine very hot. Aerial + Artillery activity normal, GONNELIEU and GOUZEAUCOURT shelled heavily by enemy. Heavy fighting on ITALIAN front - 22490 AUSTRIAN prisoners taken since 14:5:17. Lieut FRYER proceeds on leave to U.K. RBS	
	28.		Weather dull - light rain. Very little ~~[illegible]~~ artillery activity. Aerial activity on part of enemy increased. Seventeen hostile machines crossed our lines at about mid-day. Proficiency pay - CLASS II granted to one man. 2 O.R. return to duty. Two O.R. evacuated. RBS	

A7092). Wt. W12839/M1293 750,000. 1/17. D. D & L., Ltd. Forms/C2118/14.

Instructions regarding War Diaries and Intelligence Summaries are contained in F. S. Regs., Part II. and the Staff Manual respectively. Title pages will be prepared in manuscript.

VOLUME 12

MAY 1917

WAR DIARY

~~or~~

~~INTELLIGENCE SUMMARY.~~

(Erase heading not required.)

Army Form C. 2118.

120th MACHINE GUN COY.

Place	Date	Hour	Summary of Events and Information	Remarks and references to Appendices
W.12.b.6.9.	29.		Weather fine. Artillery activity normal. Hostile aeroplanes very active. One M.G. shifted out of front line to new position at about R.26.b.6.2. Two guns do indirect overhead fire during night 29th/30th between 10 p.m.–10.30 p.m. & 11.30 p.m.–12.30 a.m. from R.32.b. on to roads & tracks R.22.d & R.23.c. 2000 rounds per gun fired. No retaliation. Large fire seen in direction of LA VACQUERIE at 1.45 a.m. One O.R. proceeds on leave to U.K. One O.R. returns to duty. RGS	
	30.		Weather fine. Artillery and aerial activity below normal. Three O.R. return to duty. RGS	
	31.		Work – making shelters W.12.b.6.9. Weather fine. Artillery & aerial activity normal. RGS	

R.G. Scott. Lt.
for O.C.
120th M.G. Coy.

A7092). Wt. W12839/M1293 750,000. 1/17. D. D & L., Ltd. Forms/C2118/14.

Instructions regarding War Diaries and Intelligence Summaries are contained in F. S. Regs., Part II. and the Staff Manual respectively. Title pages will be prepared in manuscript.

VOLUME. 13.

WAR DIARY
or
~~INTELLIGENCE SUMMARY.~~
(Erase heading not required.)

Vol 13

Army Form C. 2118.

JUNE 1917 — 120th MACHINE GUN COY.

Place	Date 1917. JUNE.	Hour	Summary of Events and Information	Remarks and references to Appendices
W.6.d.6.0.	1.		Weather fine. aeroplane + artillery activity normal. Our artillery commence programme of concentrations which are to be carried out daily. During absence on leave of MAJOR-GEN. H. G. RUGGLES-BRISE, Brigadier-Gen. The Hon. C. S. H. DRUMMOND-WILLOUGHBY assumes command of 40th Div. + Lieut.-Col. D. H. A. DICK takes command of 120th Inf Bde. RGS	
	2		Indirect overhead fire carried out with two M.G. on night of 1st/2nd between 10.15 + 10.45 p.m. and 11.45 pm + 12.15 a.m. - Targets SONNET FARM and roads and tracks R.23.a. + R.22.c. - 2000 rounds per gun. Enemy artillery active - shelling about W.6.d from mid-day to about 5 p.m. Weather - light rain 1 p.m. to 7 p.m. Aerial activity normal. 2nd Lt. BENNETT proceeds on leave to U.K. RGS	
	3.		Weather fine. Enemy shelling intermittently throughout the day batteries about W.6.a and X.1.c. During the day, enemy aeroplanes were active. Our machines doing night flying from 10 p.m. One O.R. wounded. RGS	
	4.		Weather fine - enemy shelling battery W.6.a from 9.15 a.m till about 12 noon. "S.O.S" signal put up by a Battn. on our left to EAST of VILLERS-PLOUICH at 2.15 a.m (5th) in consequence of raid by enemy - heavy artillery bombardment on our front line here till 2.30 a.m (5th). The raid was unsuccessful - enemy failing to reach our trenches. Our aircraft very active - hostile aerial activity below normal. Notice received that 2nd Lt ROSKIN, evacuated to U.K. on 26.5.17. RGS	
	5.		One O.R. proceeds on leave to U.K. Weather fine - very hot. Artillery and aerial activity normal. RGS	

A7092). Wt. W12839/M1293 750,000. 1/17. D. D. & L., Ltd. Forms/C2118/14.

Instructions regarding War Diaries and Intelligence Summaries are contained in F. S. Regs., Part II. and the Staff Manual respectively. Title pages will be prepared in manuscript.

VOLUME. 13.

WAR DIARY
or
~~INTELLIGENCE~~ SUMMARY.
(Erase heading not required.)

Army Form C. 2118.

JUNE 1917. 120th MACHINE GUN COY.

Place	Date	Hour	Summary of Events and Information	Remarks and references to Appendices
	1917 JUNE			
W.6.d.6.0	6.		One O.R. returns from leave. 1 O.R. reports as reinforcement. 1 O.R. accidentally wounded. Intense bombardment by our Artillery from 5 to 5.15 p.m. for purpose of getting retaliation & locating hostile batteries. Four M.Gs. co-operate - 3 firing on to roads near LE VACQUERIE & 1 on to SONNET FARM - 125 rounds per minute per gun fired - very little retaliation. Weather - fine & very hot. RBL	
	7.		Indirect overhead fire carried out on night of 7/8 - two guns fired 1000 per gun from R.26.a. - on to Road junction R.15.d.95.60 & Road R.15.d.0.6 to R.16.a.8.0 - time of firing 10.15 to 10.45 p.m. & 11.30 to 12 midnight. Hostile artillery very quiet. Weather - heavy rain 3 p.m to 5 p.m. Attack by 2nd Army commences 3.10 a.m. - British capture WITSCHAETE & MESSINES, & 5,600 prisoners. One O.R. proceeds on leave to U.K. RBL	
	8.		Weather cloudy. At 2 a.m. gas alarm sent up by Brigade on our left - cancelled shortly afterwards. Our aeroplanes very active - hostile aerial activity above normal - at 11.15 a.m. 14 enemy aeroplanes come over our lines near VILLERS GUISLAIN. Indirect fire carried out during night 8/9th between hours 10 to 10.20 p.m & 11.5 to 11.25 p.m. - 2 guns fire 1000 rounds each from R.32.b - targets, road junctions in LE VACQUERIE. One O.R. proceeds on M.G. Course at CAMIERS. Lt. ATTALE returns from course at CAMIERS. RBL	
	9.		Two O.R. return from course at CAMIERS. RBL Light rain from 3 p.m. One O.R. proceeds on leave to U.K. One O.R. returns from leave RBL	
	9.		Practically no aerial activity. Weather dull & cloudy. Indirect overhead fire carried out with two guns from R.26.a on to sunken road R.16.a.0.0 & road junction R.21.b.3.7 - firing from 11 pm to 11.15 pm & from 11.45 p.m to 12 midnight - 1000 rounds per gun. Work - made new A.A. emplacement at W.6.d.5.1. RBL	

A7092). Wt. W12839/M1293 750,000. 1/17. D. D & L., Ltd. Forms/C2118/14.

Instructions regarding War Diaries and Intelligence Summaries are contained in F. S. Regs., Part II. and the Staff Manual respectively. Title pages will be prepared in manuscript.

VOLUME 13

WAR DIARY
or
~~INTELLIGENCE SUMMARY.~~

(Erase heading not required.)

Army Form C. 2118.

JUNE 1917

120th MACHINE GUN Coy

Place	Date	Hour	Summary of Events and Information	Remarks and references to Appendices
	1917 JUNE			
W.6.b.6.0.	10.		One O.R. proceeds on leave to U.K. Brigade relief commences night of 10/11th - 120th M.G. Coy & 120th T.M.B. relieved by 121st M.G. Coy & T.M.B. respectively. 120th M.G.Coy proceed to DESSART WOOD (W.1 & 7.1), & put four guns in the BROWN or 2nd LINE. Weather dull & cloudy. Great artillery activity to SOUTH from 10pm to 11.30 pm. RLL	
DESSART WOOD. W.1.&.7.1.	11.		Relief of 120th Inf Bde by 121st Inf Bde completed on night of 11/12th. Heavy rain & thunder from 3 am to 7 am remainder of day cloudy. Coy. cleaning up guns & equipment & improving bivouacs. RLL	
	12.		Weather hot & cloudy. Parades in Morning. Recreational Training in afternoon. 1 OR proceeds on LEAVE.	
	13.		LT. FRYER returns from leave. Moved from DESSARTWOOD & pitched Camp in valley just SOUTH (W.2.C.0.5).	
	14.		One O.R. proceeds on leave to U.K. Our aeroplanes very active. Parades in morning. Recreation Training in afternoon.	
	15.		One O.R. returns from leave.	
	16.		Anniversary of Coy's landing in France; Parades in morning. Sports in afternoon. Football match v "C" Coy H.L.I. in evening. Won 1-0.	
	17.		C.O. proceeds on leave to U.K. Church Parades. LT. FRYER assumes command of Coy & reconnoitres line with view of relieving 119 Coy.	
	18.		Guns & limbers packed. Pte. Whittle remanded for F.G.C.M. Coy relieves 119 Coy in Villers Guislain sector. Four guns on rt. in front line: 3 guns on left in close support: 3 guns in FIFTEEN RAVINE. One doing A.A. work. 4 guns in Reserve at Coy H.Q. Q.29 d.2.0.	

A7092). Wt. W12839/M1293 750,000. 1/17. D. D & L., Ltd. Forms/C2118/14.

Instructions regarding War Diaries and Intelligence Summaries are contained in F. S. Regs., Part II. and the Staff Manual respectively. Title pages will be prepared in manuscript.

VOLUME 13.

JUNE 1917

WAR DIARY
or
~~INTELLIGENCE SUMMARY.~~
(Erase heading not required.)

Army Form C. 2118.

120th MACHINE GUN COMPANY.

Place	Date 1917 JUNE	Hour	Summary of Events and Information	Remarks and references to Appendices
Q.96.2.0 (Sheet 57 C S.E.2)	19th		Guns in BROWN line relieved by 119 Coy. Weather changed: dull & rainy. 120th Inf. Bde. relieve 119th Inf. Bde. in VILLERS PLUICH Sector. [illegible]	
	20th		One O.R. proceeds on leave to U.K. A.A. gun engaged enemy 'plane at 8.30 p.m. without any visible results. LONG Range gun shells VILLERS PLUICH between 4 p.m. and 6 p.m. Weather still dull & rainy. [illegible]	
	21		One O.R. returns from leave. All morning GOUZEAUCOURT shelled by enemy. Sniping gun & team sent up to VILLERS. More Rain. A.A. gun engages enemy 'plane at 8.30 p.m. without any visible result. [illegible]	
	22		One O.R. proceeds on leave & one returns. Pte. WHITTLE tried by F.G.C.M. One gun & team sent up to VILLERS to do indirect (night) fire. Weather still rainy. [illegible]	
	23rd		Sniping Machine Gun fired on parties of the Enemy in COUILLET WOOD during the day. 2 Guns carried out indirect fire on LA VACQUERIE & COUILLET WOOD after dark. 3000 Rounds expended. Our Artillery normal, hostile artillery quiet. 8.30 pm 6 hostile aeroplanes passed over our lines two were driven off by A A fire. R.J.L.	
	24th		Weather fine. Sniping Machine Gun still active firing on & dispersing enemy movement, several of the enemy seen to drop, later carried away on Stretchers. Artillery both hostile & own activity below normal	
		6.30 pm	Twelve Enemy Aeroplanes passed over our lines flying low at a great speed in S.E. direction.	

A7092). Wt. W12839/M1292 750,000. 1/17. D. D & L., Ltd. Forms/C2118/14.

Army Form C. 2118.

Instructions regarding War Diaries and Intelligence Summaries are contained in F. S. Regs., Part II. and the Staff Manual respectively. Title pages will be prepared in manuscript.

VOLUME 13

JUNE 1917

WAR DIARY
or
~~INTELLIGENCE~~ SUMMARY.
(Erase heading not required.)

120th MACHINE GUN COY.

Place	1917 Date JUNE	Hour	Summary of Events and Information	Remarks and references to Appendices
Q29 b.2.0.	24th		One O.R. proceeds to U.K. on leave. R.J.F.	
	25th	1am	Hostile raiding party, (strength unknown) bombed covering party to working party on right battalion front, Enemy retired on being fired on. Our Sniping M.G. carried out direct fire on Enemy movement during day. It has been noticed that the movements of enemy parties have been more cautious & he keeps to his trenches as much as possible. Indirect fire on tracks used by Enemy carried out during the night. Our Artillery activity normal, hostile activity very quiet. 2/Lt PAGE & C.S.M. Redman proceeded on 4th Army Infy School course at FLIXECOURT. 2/Lt ROWLAND evacuated whilst on leave in U.K. 2 OR's admitted to hospital R.J.F.	
	26th		Weather overcast. Our Sniping Machine Gun continues to disperse parties of enemy & at night 2 guns carry out indirect fire on Enemy approaches tracks etc, average expenditure of S.A.A. per day 5000 rounds. Artillery normal. Hostile aircraft fairly active 18 hostile machines observed during the day & several O B's were up. Lieut SHARPE proceeds on leave to U.K. Major A.T. LACEY appointed Divisional M.G. officer. 1 O.R. returned from leave. R.J.F.	
	27th		Weather changeable. Hostile activity below normal. very little shelling. Gun teams in front line relieved by support & reserve sections.	
	28th		Lieut SCOTT returns from leave. 1 O.R. proceeds on leave. Sniping carried out by day with M.G. resulted in keeping enemy movement down. several hits claimed. Indirect fire on GOODMAN FARM & LA VACQUERIE at night. Enemy reported to be working on his wire, & improving trenches. Hostile artillery more active than usual, back areas being shelled. R.J.F.	

A5834 Wt. W4973/M687 750,000 8/16 D. D. & L. Ltd. Forms/C.2118/13.

Army Form C. 2118.

Instructions regarding War Diaries and Intelligence Summaries are contained in F. S. Regs., Part II. and the Staff Manual respectively. Title pages will be prepared in manuscript.

VOLUME 13

JUNE 1917

WAR DIARY or ~~INTELLIGENCE~~ SUMMARY.

(Erase heading not required.)

120th MACHINE GUN COMPANY.

Place	Date	Hour	Summary of Events and Information	Remarks and references to Appendices
Q29b2.0.	29th		Weather Changeable. Situation normal. Sniping & Indirect Fire Machine Guns carried out fire on Enemy movement by day & tracks, Roads etc by night. Bombardment of our front line on Rt Sector about 12 midnight. Enemy using Searchlight from direction of BLEAK HOUSE. R.G.J.	
	30th		Weather Rainy very dull. Situation normal. Hostile & own artillery quiet. MG Sniping Gun in action during day, a few hits claimed, owing to rain, very little enemy movement observed in front system. 1 O.R. interviewed by G.O.C. 121 Inf Bde with a view to obtaining Temp. Commission. 1 O.R. proceeded to UK on leave. R.G.J.	

R.G. Fryer Lieut
O.C. 120 Machine Gun Coy

A5834 Wt. W4973/M687 750,000 8/16 D. D. & L. Ltd. Forms/C.2118/13.

Instructions regarding War Diaries and Intelligence Summaries are contained in F. S. Regs., Part II. and the Staff Manual respectively. Title pages will be prepared in manuscript.

VOLUME 14.

JULY 1917

WAR DIARY or INTELLIGENCE SUMMARY.

(Erase heading not required.)

Army Form C. 2118.

Vol 14

120th MACHINE GUN COMPANY

Place	Date	Hour	Summary of Events and Information	Remarks and references to Appendices
Q.24.c.2.0. (57c S.E.2.)	1st		Weather fine. Our Sniping Machine Gun fired on movement in vicinity of HINDENBURG support line & COUILLET WOOD during the day. Indirect fire on Roads & tracks reported to be used by enemy fired on during night. Our artillery [illegible] PENELOSSE & COUILLET WOOD in retaliation to hostile shelling of GONNELIEU & TWENTY TWO RAVINE. Considerable movement observed behind enemies lines. RGY	
		1.40pm	E.A. flew over VILLERS PLOUICH very low down on being fired on by M.G. quickly made off. 1 O.R. wounded. 1 O.R. returned from M.G. Course.	
	2nd		Hostile activity below normal. Our Sniping M.G. carried out sniping on usual targets & Indirect fire at night. 1 O.R. returned from Hospital. 1 Officer (Lieut ATTALE) proceeded to U.K. on leave. RGY	
	3rd		Weather unsettled fine. Inter section relief carried out. Situation quiet, usual movement fired on by Sniping Gun. Indirect fire carried out during night.	
		4pm	E.A. attempted to bring down our O.B. at HEUDECOURT but was brought down by machine gun fire. During a fight with an enemy plane one of our machines was brought down at W.2.d.5.0. Bombs dropped by E.A. over SOREL-LE-GRAND & GOUZEAUCOURT. RGY	
	4th		Hostile artillery fairly active. VILLERS PLOUICH & GOUZEAUCOURT being shelled. Considerable movement in COUILLET WOOD fired on by Sniping M.Gun. Notice board fixed in front of GERMAN wire reads POOR LITTLE BANTAM. M.G. emplacements in the Intermediate line improved. 1 O.R. returned from leave. 1 O.R. proceeded on leave. RGY	
	5th		Hostile artillery very active during the day, shelling our front line defences.	
		11.30pm	Enemy raiding party attempted to reach our lines but were driven off by rifle & M.G. fire. Indirect M.G. fire & Sniping M.G. withdrawn ~~temporarily~~ as Enemy retaliated with his M.G. RGY	

A5834 Wt. W4973/M687 750,000 8/16 D. D. & L. Ltd. Forms/C.2118/13.

VOLUME 14.

Instructions regarding War Diaries and Intelligence Summaries are contained in F. S. Regs., Part II. and the Staff Manual respectively. Title pages will be prepared in manuscript.

WAR DIARY
or
~~INTELLIGENCE SUMMARY.~~

(Erase heading not required.)

Army Form C. 2118.

JULY 1917. 120th MACHINE GUN COY

Place	Date	Hour	Summary of Events and Information	Remarks and references to Appendices
Q29 b.2.0 (Sheet 57c S.E.)	6th		Hostile artillery active our front system being heavily shelled. Own artillery retaliated. Considerable movement observed behind enemies lines. Aviation quiet during day more active towards the evening. 1 OR proceeded on leave to U.K. 1 OR returned from leave. R.J.F.	
	7th		Hostile artillery & T.M's very active all day shelling our front system & destroying our wire, a hostile raid expected on a fairly large scale, necessary precautions taken an extra M.G put in front line in R.T. Bde's area where it could enfilade our wire. ~~two~~ front line M.G's withdrawn to Reserve at 15 Ravine. Night passed quietly no hostile action taken. Enemy aviation active, one enemy ~~[illegible]~~ E.A. attacked one of our O.B's near HAVRINCOURT & brought it down. 120th Brigade H.Q. move up to CEASARS CAMP (Q29 b 2.1) 2 O.R. detained in Hospital.	R.J.F.
	8th		Our front line heavily bombarded during the day. Own artillery retaliated. Considerable enemy movement observed. Hostile aircraft again very active especially during the bombardment. 1 O.R proceeded on leave. 1 OR returned from leave. R.J.F.	
	9th		Hostile Artillery again very active GONNELIEU receiving especial attention. Own Artillery concentrated on enemies Trench System. Enemy Snipers & M.G's fairly active. Reserve M.G. Section moved from Q29 b.2.0. to BROWN LINE. Five new positions reconnoitred on right of intermediate line, these are being constructed by R.E. and will be occupied by guns of this Company on completion. ~~Lieut~~ Lieut SHARPE returned from leave. 1 OR detained in Hospital. R.J.F.	
	10th		Hostile Artillery still very active. Hostile M.G's swept No mans land during the night. Aviation very quiet. Usual movement seen behind enemies lines. 1 OR returned from hospital. R.J.F.	

A5834 Wt. W4973/M687 750,000 8/16 D. D. & L. Ltd. Forms/C.2118/13.

Instructions regarding War Diaries and Intelligence Summaries are contained in F. S. Regs., Part II. and the Staff Manual respectively. Title pages will be prepared in manuscript.

VOLUME 14

WAR DIARY
or
INTELLIGENCE SUMMARY.
(*Erase heading not required.*)

Army Form C. 2118.

JULY 1917 — 120th MACHINE GUN COY.

Place	Date	Hour	Summary of Events and Information	Remarks and references to Appendices
Q29 b20	11th		Hostile artillery quiet during the day, but opened an intense bombardment on Rt Bn front between 1.35am & 2.15am: on SOS being sent up, our M.G.'s opened fire. no hostile action followed: 1 OR returned from leave. Divisional Horse show held, 1st prize for limber & pair of mules won by this Coy. RJL	
	12th	11.30pm	Hostile Artillery less active. Own artillery carried out concentrations & shelled movement which was fairly considerable. Right & Left Bns carried out minor operations for the purpose of obtaining identification, 2 of our M.G.'s were in position to fire on Enemy Strong Point, to engage enemies trenches on S.E. flank of Raiding party, but owing to the thickness of the wire the operation was cancelled. Left Battalion were more successful after blowing a gap in enemies wire by means of a Bangalore entered enemy trenches but failed to take a prisoner, our M.G.'s were to fire if called upon, but were not required. this company had one casualty (wounded) 2 OR admitted to hospital. RJL	
	13th		Hostile Artillery remarkably quiet. Own artillery shelled enemies trenches & dispersed parties moving behind lines. 2 machine guns have been moved up into VILLERS PLOUICH for the purpose of sniping by day & indirect fire by night. 1 officer 2/Lt THAMS reported from Base as reinforcement. RJL	
	14th		Hostile Artillery still very quiet. Our Sniping M. Gun dispersed several parties of the Enemy during the day. Indirect fire on tracks GOOD MAN FARM & COUILLET WOOD during the night. 2 OR returned to duty, one from hospital & one from Brigade. Considerable aircraft activity during the day. RJL	

A5834 Wt. W4973/M687 750,000 8/16 D. D. & L. Ltd. Forms/C.2118/13.

Instructions regarding War Diaries and Intelligence Summaries are contained in F. S. Regs., Part II. and the Staff Manual respectively. Title pages will be prepared in manuscript.

VOLUME 14

JULY 1917

WAR DIARY
or
INTELLIGENCE SUMMARY.

(Erase heading not required.)

120th MACHINE GUN Coy

Army Form C. 2118.

Place	Date	Hour	Summary of Events and Information	Remarks and references to Appendices
Q29b.2.0. (57c.S.E.2)	15th		Our artillery active during day, enemies reply weak. GOUZEAUCOURT & GONNELIEU being lightly shelled. Considerable movement seen on Roads & in the trenches over [illegible] M Gun in action during hours of daylight. 1 OR proceeds on leave. RPT.	
	16th		Hostile artillery fairly active. [illegible] M.G. dispersed & [illegible] movement in areas R2 & R3. Indirect fire carried out during night. Considerable aircraft activity during the day about 6.30pm 2 E.A. attempted to bring down one of our O.B's but were driven off by M.G. & A.A. fire. RPT	
	17th		Hostile artillery active against batteries in GOUZEAUCOURT WOOD. Aerial activity below normal. Indirect fire carried out during night. W.P.H.	
	18th		Artillery activity normal during day but increased towards evening. Our light forces in NORTH SEA capture 4 German ships. French advance 2½ miles to depth of 1 kilometre. W.P.H.	
	19th		1 OR returns from leave. Div M.G. [illegible]. Indirect fire during night. Hostile artillery active. W.P.H.	
	20th		1 OR returns from leave. Div [illegible] immediately North of [illegible] 2 [illegible]. [illegible] unsuccessful attempt to raid enemy strong post. W.P.H.	
	21st		Internal relief of 3 guns in VILLERS PLOUICH. 1 OR wounded. No indirect fire : Batt[illegible] were carrying out relief. No S.O.S. [illegible]. 1 German officer & about 12 OR. made their way into our front line about 6pm. & escaped again. W.P.H.	
	22nd		Great aerial activity both our own & enemy. 3 guns in Right Sector relieved.	

A5834 Wt. W4973/M687 750,000 8/16 D. D. & L. Ltd. Forms/C.2118/13.

Army Form C. 2118.

Instructions regarding War Diaries and Intelligence Summaries are contained in F. S. Regs., Part II. and the Staff Manual respectively. Title pages will be prepared in manuscript.

VOLUME 14

JULY 1917

WAR DIARY
or
~~INTELLIGENCE SUMMARY.~~
(Erase heading not required.)

Place	Date	Hour	Summary of Events and Information	Remarks and references to Appendices
Q29 b.2.D (7C.S.E.2)	23rd		Artillery: both our own & enemy, Normal. Hostile planes very active. Indirect Fire guns fired on selected targets during night. FRENCH heavily bombarded in region of HURTEBISE - CRAONNE but two GERMAN attacks successful. German aeroplanes raided FELIXSTOWE and HARWICH. 1 O.R. detained in Hospital.	
	24th		Artillery: enemy quiet except for a little counter battery work, Ours Normal. Indirect Fire guns fired during night. BRIGADE immediately N. carry out successful raid. FRENCH still heavily bombarded in region of HURTEBISE and CHAMPAGNE. Russian situation [illegible]. Cpl. BROWN transferred from 121 Coy.	
	25th		ARTILLERY: both ours & enemy normal. Our planes very active. Our 2 guns carried out indirect fire during night.	
	26th	6 a.m.	ARTILLERY: ours normal, enemy very active on right sector. Enemy planes also very active. BRIGADE S. of us successfully raided by enemy in daylight. 1 O.R. proceeds to Cadet school U.K. Sgt. BENNETT & 3 O.R. proceed to CAMIERS. 1 O.R. proceeds on leave to U.K. 1 O.R. returns from Hospital. HEAVY fighting in region of HURTEBISE. Armed Cruiser "OTWAY" & submarine C34 torpedoed in NORTH SEA. Increase in number of ships torpedoed.	
	27th		ARTILLERY: Normal. Aerial activity: NORMAL. 2 new positions made in right section & 2 guns put there to help artillery barrage. Now have FIVE guns in [illegible] & THREE in LEFT [illegible]. S.O.S. lines altered to fit in with Artillery.	
	28th		ARTILLERY: Normal. Enemy planes very active during morning. 1 O.R. [illegible] M.G. 1 O.R. returns from Hospital: 1 O.R. returns from Leave.	
	29th		ARTILLERY: normal. AERIAL activity above normal. H.L.I. attempt to raid FARM TRENCH but were frustrated by hostile patrol. GERMAN raiding party twice driven off from ROPE AVENUE. Sgt. TYDDLESLEY applied for by [illegible] leaves for BASE.	
	30th		ARTILLERY: Normal. Air below normal. Carried out inter-section relief. Corps sports at Corps HQ.	
	31st		ARTILLERY: below normal. No air. Weather too dull. R.F.A. sports at EQUANCOURT.	[signature] Lieut. O.C. 120th M.G. Coy.

A5834 Wt. W4973/M687 750,000 8/16 D. D. & L. Ltd. Forms/C.2118/13.

Instructions regarding War Diaries and Intelligence Summaries are contained in F. S. Regs., Part II. and the Staff Manual respectively. Title pages will be prepared in manuscript.

VOLUME 15

WAR DIARY
or
~~INTELLIGENCE SUMMARY.~~
(Erase heading not required.)

Army Form C. 2118.

Vol 15

August 1917. 120th Machine Gun Coy

Place	Date	Hour	Summary of Events and Information	Remarks and references to Appendices
CAESAR'S CAMP	AUG. 1st		Artillery: Normal. Aerial Activity: Below normal. British with French on left attacked on wide front North of River LYS. Advanced from one to two miles on fifteen mile front.	W.J.E.A.
Q.29.B.2.0. (57C.S.E.²)	2nd		Artillery: Normal. Aerial Activity: Below normal. Hostile Counter attacks successfully repulsed in Flanders. Dinᵗ CoY 2U4 Relieved 4 guns in intermediate line. These 4 guns relieve 4 guns of 27 M.G. CoY in S.O.S. positions behind BEAUCAMP. W.J.E.A.	
Q.18.B.70.90	3rd		Artillery: Below Normal. A.A. Below normal. Company Hd.Qrs. moved to Q.18.B.70.90.	
		11 pm	guns in Right Sector relieved by 119 M.G. CoY. Four guns from Brown Line relieve	
		2.pm	27 M.G. CoY in front line in front of BEAUCAMP. Eleven guns now in line, because Brigade side stepped & 3 left guns remained in, becoming 3 right guns. Hostile raid attempted during Infantry relief. Successfully beaten off. Change in weather. Rain.	W.J.E.A.
			1 O.R. proceeded to ALBERT on Cookery Class. 2/LT. PAGE returns from Course with C.S.M. REDMAN & 1 O.R. Pte BROWN appointed unpaid L/Cpl from 24/7/17. W.J.E.A.	
	4th		Artillery: below normal. A.A. below normal. Hostile counterattacks N.E. of YPRES unsuccessful. Austrians capture CZERNOWITZ. W.J.E.A.	
	5th		Artillery: very quiet. A.A. below normal. British recapture ST. JULIEN VILLAGE from which they were driven on Aug. 1st.	
			~~BEGINNING of FOURTH year of WAR.~~	W.J.E.A.

A7092). Wt. W12839/M1293. 750,000. 1/17. D. D & L., Ltd. Forms/C2118/14.

Army Form C. 2118.

WAR DIARY
or
~~INTELLIGENCE SUMMARY.~~
(Erase heading not required.)

Instructions regarding War Diaries and Intelligence Summaries are contained in F. S. Regs., Part II. and the Staff Manual respectively. Title pages will be prepared in manuscript.

VOLUME 15 — August 1917. — 120 Machine Gun Coy

Place	Date	Hour	Summary of Events and Information	Remarks and references to Appendices
Q.18.d.70.90	Aug 6th		Artillery: ours normal. enemy's very quiet. Enemy Aeroplanes very active during afternoon & evening, 1 airman going during display of clever flying over our front line despite AA & Lewis Gun fire. 2 OR. admitted to hospital sick. 1 OR. proceeded on Leave. [initials] under heavy mist & without bombardment enemy try daylight raid on GILLEMONT. [initials]	
	7th		Artillery: fairly active. Enemy aeroplane activity increased. 2 bombs dropped on FINS. Enemy lamp-signalling from CAMBRAI to Q.6.b. Eight loud explosions heard in BANTEUX.	[initials]
	8th		Artillery: ours quiet. Enemy's much above normal. VILLERS GUISLAIN received several H.V. naval shells. Aerial Activity: None. 1. OR. returns from Leave. [initials]	
	9.		Weather unsettled - intermittent showers. Artillery & aerial activity both ours & enemy below normal. LT. ATTALE wounded (admitted to C.C.S) & 1 O.R. Killed by bomb dropped from aeroplane. 1 OR. proceeds on leave. [initials]	
	10.		Work proceeding on two new emplacements & shelters in front line: about Q.7.a & Q.12.a. [initials] Weather cleared up. Aerial activity increased on both sides. Enemy artillery active on our front & support lines about Q.12.c & R.7 and elsewhere. Considerable retaliation by our Artillery. Work proceeding on emplacements & shelters [initials]	
	11.		Weather - raining on & off - our & enemy aerial & artillery activity below normal. Work proceeding on emplacements & shelters [initials]	
	12.		Weather - wet - very cloudy - very little aerial or artillery activity. 1 OR. wounded. 1 OR. admitted to hospital. 1 OR. proceeds on leave. Work proceeding on emplacements, shelters & Section Headquarters at Q.12.d. [initials]	

A7092). Wt. W12839/M1293 750,000. 1/17. D. D & L., Ltd. Forms/C2118/14.

Army Form C. 2118.

WAR DIARY
~~or~~
~~INTELLIGENCE SUMMARY~~.
(Erase heading not required.)

Instructions regarding War Diaries and Intelligence Summaries are contained in F. S. Regs., Part II. and the Staff Manual respectively. Title pages will be prepared in manuscript.

VOLUME 15.

August 1917.

120th MACHINE GUN COY.

Place	Date	Hour	Summary of Events and Information	Remarks and references to Appendices
Q. 8. b. 7. 9.	1917 August 13.		Weather - raining nearly all day. Our own & hostile artillery very quiet. Our aerial activity normal. In evening, considerable enemy aerial activity. A. A. M.G. fired 800 rounds from Q. 12. d. b. 1. One O.R. admitted to hospital. RGS.	
	14.		Weather fine. Reconnoitred position for M.G. in sector of Division on left. Our own & hostile artillery activity below normal. Aerial activity above normal during the latter part of the afternoon. One O.R. proceeds on leave. RGS.	
	15.		Weather - showers during afternoon & throughout night of 15/16th. Artillery & aerial activity much below normal. Lieut. BERKELEY. P.C.O. reported as a reinforcement. Sgt POWER proceeds to join No. 21 M.G. Coy as C.Q.M.S. One M.G. moved from Q.12. a. 35.90 to Q.11. b. 5. 8. Lt. FRYER promoted Acting Capt. whilst commanding Coy. RGS.	
	16.		Weather fine. Hostile aerial & artillery activity below normal. Our own & enemy aeroplanes very active during latter part of afternoon. RGS. Internal relief at emplacements M.G.1 & M.G.2. RGS.	
	17.		Weather fine. Artillery quiet. Hostile aeroplanes very active during the morning. RGS. One O.R. evacuated. RGS.	
	18.		Weather fine. Two guns do indirect fire from Q.18. b. 4.3 between 9.30 pm. & midnight on to trenches, roads & tracks about R.1.a. R.1.b. & R.2.a. - 2000 rounds per gun. Our own & hostile artillery & aerial activity normal. RGS.	
	19.		Weather fine. Artillery (our own & enemy) very quiet. Aerial activity normal. RGS.	

A7092). Wt. W12839/M1293 750,000. 1/17. D. D & L., Ltd. Forms/C2118/14.

Army Form C. 2118.

Instructions regarding War Diaries and Intelligence Summaries are contained in F. S. Regs., Part II. and the Staff Manual respectively. Title pages will be prepared in manuscript.

VOLUME. 15.

August 1917.

WAR DIARY

~~or~~

~~INTELLIGENCE SUMMARY.~~

(Erase heading not required.)

120th Machine Gun Coy.

Place	Date	Hour	Summary of Events and Information	Remarks and references to Appendices
	1917 August.			
Q.8.b.7.9.	20.		Weather fine. Two guns do indirect fire from Q.18.b.4.3. between 9 p.m + midnight, on to trenches, roads + tracks about R.1.a, R.1.b. + R.2.a. - 2000 rounds per gun. One O.R. returns from leave. Artillery & aerial activity normal. RGL	
	21.		Weather fine. A similar programme of indirect fire carried out as during previous night. Enemy aircraft very active during morning up till midday. Hostile artillery quiet. One O.R. reports as reinforcement. RGL	
	22.		Weather very hot - fine. Enemy aerial activity above normal, artillery quiet. RGL	
	23.		Weather fine. Two guns, fire 4000 rounds on to roads & new trenches about K.35.d & Q.6.b. between 10 p.m + 4 am (24th) (indirect). Artillery & aerial activity on both sides normal. One O.R. evacuated. 2 O.R. report from hospital. 2 O.R. report as reinforcements. 1 O.R. returns from leave. RGL	
	24.		Weather fine. During night (24th/25th) seven Vickers guns and Lewis guns carried out a combined shoot sweeping NO MANS LAND & enemy parapet. 1400 rounds fired from Vickers guns. Hostile artillery activity normal. Hostile aerial activity below normal. RGL.	
	25.		Weather fine. About 6 a.m. a small party of enemy found in our front line trench about R.7.a. were speedily dislodged leaving one prisoner. This prisoner stated that our machine gun fire was accurate, but few casualties	

A7092). Wt. W12839/M1293. 750,000. 1/17. D. D & L., Ltd. Forms/C2118/14.

Instructions regarding War Diaries and Intelligence Summaries are contained in F. S. Regs., Part II. and the Staff Manual respectively. Title pages will be prepared in manuscript.

VOLUME 15.

WAR DIARY

~~or~~

~~INTELLIGENCE SUMMARY~~.

(Erase heading not required.)

Army Form C. 2118.

August 1917.

120th MACHINE GUN COY.

Place	Date	Hour	Summary of Events and Information	Remarks and references to Appendices
	1917. August.			
Q.8.b.7.9.	25 (Con).		were caused by it, owing to the dangerous spots being avoided by the enemy. One O.R. proceeds on leave. 1 officer + 3 O.R. return from course at CAMIERS. Practically no hostile aerial activity. About 2000 rounds fired from two Vickers guns in front line on to German front line about R.1.d & R.8.a. RGL	
	26.		Weather fine. Practically no aerial activity. Artillery on both sides quiet. One O.R. returns from course on Cookery. RGL 3 O.R. proceed on leave. RGL	
	27.		Internal Coy. reliefs at S.1, S2, S3 & R3. RGL Weather raining – from midday – turning cold. Enemy artillery more active than usual. Our artillery ~~[illegible]~~ normal. Our aeroplanes very active. One O.R. proceeds on leave. RGL One O.R. reports from hospital. Lieut. OLIVER-THOMPSON reports to take command of Coy. One O.R. reports as reinforcement. Internal relief at M.G.4, M.G.5 & M.G.6. RGL	
	28.		Weather – raining – light showers during afternoon ~~[illegible] midday~~ Strong wind blowing from S.S.E. Aerial activity practically nil. Artillery normal. RGL	
	29.		Weather cold & dull – strong wind blowing from S.S.E. Attending conference with C.O. 14 A & S.H. discussing proposed minor operation. Aerial activity practically nil. RGL	
	30.		Weather cold – showers during whole day. Aerial activity much below normal. One O.R. proceeds on M.G. course to CAMIERS. 2 O.R. report from leave. RGL	

A7092). Wt. W12839/M1293. 750,000. 1/17. D. D & L., Ltd. Forms/C2118/14.

Army Form C. 2118.

WAR DIARY

or

~~INTELLIGENCE SUMMARY.~~

(Erase heading not required.)

Instructions regarding War Diaries and Intelligence Summaries are contained in F. S. Regs., Part II. and the Staff Manual respectively. Title pages will be prepared in manuscript.

VOLUME. 15.

August 1917

120th Machine Gun Coy.

Place	Date	Hour	Summary of Events and Information	Remarks and references to Appendices
	1917 August.			
Q. 8. 6. 7. 9.	31.		Weather cold - showers on and off. Aerial activity practically nil. At present there is great activity to group machine guns and make them more an arm of the artillery with three S.O.S. lines. The machine gun barrage has proved most successful in recent attacks, and is now being greatly developed.	

R L Scott Lt.
for O.C.
120th M. G. Coy.

A7092). Wt. W12839/M1293 750,000. 1/17. D. D & L., Ltd. Forms/C2118/14.

Instructions regarding War Diaries and Intelligence Summaries are contained in F. S. Regs., Part II. and the Staff Manual respectively. Title pages will be prepared in manuscript.

VOLUME 16

WAR DIARY
or
~~INTELLIGENCE SUMMARY.~~
(Erase heading not required.)

Vol 16

Army Form C. 2118.

September 1917

120th MACHINE GUN COY.

Place	Date 1917 Sept.	Hour	Summary of Events and Information	Remarks and references to Appendices
Q.8.b.7.9.	1.		Weather cold. During night (1/2nd) two M.Gs fired from R.14.a in cooperation with Artillery on to track R.3.d.3.0 to R.3.b.9.0. - 4000 rounds fired. Aerial activity nil. Hostile artillery shelled BEAUCAMP - VILLERS PLOUICH road Q.12.d. about 11 a.m & 5 p.m. Two O.R. return from Farriery Course. RGS	
	2.		Weather fine. Hostile artillery shelled this brigade front more than usually. Hostile aerial activity below normal. One O.R. reports as reinforcement. RGS	
	3.		Weather fine. In view of relief, taking O.C. 244 M.G.Coy around positions. Conference at Headquarters 14th Arg & S. Hrs. re minor operation to be carried out by that Batt. During night (3/4th) one gun fired intermittently from 11 p.m. on to new German trench in course of construction about R.2.b. One OR evacuated to Hospital. RGS	
	4.		Weather hot. Section Officers 244 M.G.Coy. look around positions. One O.R. proceeds on leave. Hostile aerial activity above normal. Hostile artillery normal. Two M.Gs fired from R.14.a (5000 rounds) in cooperation with Artillery during night (4/5th) on to centre of activity R.9.b.7.8. RGS	
	5.		Weather hot. Perusing report on inspection of Transport by D.A.D.V.S. & O.C. Div. Train, which took place on 31.8.17. Report stated vehicles & harness in good & serviceable condition - more attention should be given to greasing of wheels. Animals in good condition. Hostile aerial activity much above normal. Hostile artillery activity normal. RGS	
	6		Weather - storm from 2 a.m. to 3 a.m. Hostile Artillery & aerial activity normal. On night of 6/7th 120th M.G.Coy. relieved by 244 M.G.Coy. Operation Order No 37 (Relief) annexed. RGS	

A7092). Wt. W12839/M1293. 750,000. 1/17. D. D & L., Ltd. Forms/C2118/14.

VOLUME 16.

WAR DIARY
or
INTELLIGENCE SUMMARY.
(Erase heading not required.)

Army Form C. 2118.

Instructions regarding War Diaries and Intelligence Summaries are contained in F. S. Regs., Part II. and the Staff Manual respectively. Title pages will be prepared in manuscript.

September 1917 — 120 MACHINE GUN Coy

Place	Date	Hour	Summary of Events and Information	Remarks and references to Appendices
Q86.7.9.	1917 Sept 6-7		14th A.&S.H. attempted a raid on enemy's trenches at R8d 05.95 under cover of M.G. & STOKES barrage but were unsuccessful. 4 guns of this Coy assisted in the barrage. RGJ	
HEUDECOURT	7th		Company moved into billets at HEUDECOURT for 16 days rest. Cleaning & overhauling guns & equipment. Section Officers & NCO's reconnoitre Brown line as Coy will have to occupy positions in this line in case of attack. 1 OR proceeds on leave. 1 OR to Transport Course. RGJ	
	8th		Church parades. Lieut R.G. SCOTT transferred to 103 Machine Gun Coy as 2nd in Command. 2/Lt PAGE proceeds on leave. 1 OR returned from leave. RGJ	
	9th		Company commenced training in Machine Gun Battery & Barrage Drill. 2 OR admitted to hospital. 1 man returned from Hospital. RGJ	
	10th		Company training in Barrage drill & Battery fire continued. Recreational training carried out during afternoon. Revolver practice for NCO's. 1 OR Returned from leave 1 OR proceeded on leave 1 OR from Hospital. RGJ	
	11th		Route march from 9-12.30 pm. 2.30-3.30 Box Respirator drill. CQMS to course of Cattering. Major A.T. LACEY transferred to 244 M.G. Coy as O.C. Capt OLIVER THOMPSON assumes command of 120 M.G. Coy. 2 OR from leave. RGJ	

VOLUME 16

WAR DIARY
or
~~INTELLIGENCE~~ SUMMARY.
(Erase heading not required.)

Army Form C. 2118.

Instructions regarding War Diaries and Intelligence Summaries are contained in F. S. Regs., Part II. and the Staff Manual respectively. Title pages will be prepared in manuscript.

SEPTEMBER 1917 — 120 MACHINE GUN Coy

Place	Date Sep	Hour	Summary of Events and Information	Remarks and references to Appendices
HEUDECOURT	12th		Company training & training for sports. Tactical scheme for Officers M.G's in advanced Guard action. 1 OR on Leave 1 OR evacuated to U.K. sick. 2 OR transferred to 244 M.G. Coy Hostile aeroplane passed over flying high at about 4.30 pm engaged with A.A fire RJ	
	13th		M.G 30x Range practice. Junior N.C.O's instructed under C.S.M Recreational training during afternoon RJ	
	14th		1 Officer (2/Lt Ld PELHAM) reported as reinforcement. 1 OR evacuated 1 OR returned from Leave. Coy practised M.G. Battery drill. Fatigue party of 8 men to be supplied to Town Major daily. RJ	
	15th		Church Parades. CQMS returned from course of Catering 1 OR from Hospital 1 OR evacuated RJ	
	16th		Company training Semaphore M.G. Battery drill. R.T. 1 OR Evacuated. 1 OR from Hospital. Orders received that 14 HLI will carry out minor enterprise on night 21st/22nd M.G's will cooperate, this Company to provide 8 Guns for barrage. RJ	
	17th		Company training M.G. & Range taking RJ	
	18th		Company Sports. 1 OR from Leave 4 OR to Divisional ~~[illegible]~~ signal Course at NURLU RJ	
	19th		Cleaning & preparing guns & equipment ready to go up the line 1 OR admitted to Hospital RJ	

Army Form C. 2118.

Instructions regarding War Diaries and Intelligence Summaries are contained in F. S. Regs., Part II. and the Staff Manual respectively. Title pages will be prepared in manuscript.

VOLUME 16

WAR DIARY
or
INTELLIGENCE SUMMARY.
(Erase heading not required.)

SEPTEMBER 1917

120 MACHINE GUN COY

Place	Date 1917	Hour	Summary of Events and Information	Remarks and references to Appendices
HEUDECOURT	Sept 20th		3 officers & Nos 1 & 2 Sections go up to BEAUCAMP to prepare positions & work out barrage lines for operations on night 21/22nd. Coy Concert in the Evening. Remainder of Coy carry out training in Barrage & Battery work. RJB	
	21st		Remainder of Coy go for Route March. afternoon Football match	
			Operations for 21/22nd night postponed owing to an unfavourable wind. Weather good.	RJB
Q12 d. 10.05	22nd		Nos. 3 & 4 Sections & Hdqrs. prepared guns etc. & cleaned Billets preparatory to going into the Line. At 8 p.m. they left Heudicourt & the Company relieved 244 M.G. Coy. later.	
GOUZEAUCOURT 1/20000			Nos. 1 & 2 Sections prepared for operations ordered & in conjunction with other Coys. put down a successful Barrage on either side of VILLERS VALLEY about in line with S. edge of PINECORPSE. The raid was successful & the Coy. had no casualties. 1 O.R. returned from Hospital. Weather good	Ref. GOUZEAUCOURT 1/20000 Fired 40000 rds. RJB
	23rd		1 O.R. proceeded on leave. 2/Lt. PAGE returned from Leave. Front quiet. Weather good.	
	24th		2 Guns fired during the night at Targets in R15 b & R15 d. Front quiet. Weather good 1 O.R. returned from Hospital. RJB	Ref above MAP.
	25th		Raid by 121 Bde. on BLEAK TRENCH. 2 of our M. Guns fired during the night at the points damaged during the 120 Bde. raid. Weather good. Front quiet. RJB	

Army Form C. 2118.

VOLUME 16

WAR DIARY
~~or~~
~~INTELLIGENCE SUMMARY.~~
(Erase heading not required.)

Instructions regarding War Diaries and Intelligence Summaries are contained in F. S. Regs., Part II. and the Staff Manual respectively. Title pages will be prepared in manuscript.

SEPTEMBER 1917 — 120 MACHINE GUN COMPANY

Place	Date	Hour	Summary of Events and Information	Remarks and references to Appendices
Q12 d 60.05	26th		Situation quiet. Weather still excellent. 2 O.R. Reinforcements. RWB.	
	27th		Hostile Artillery busy – nearly accounted for Coy. Hdqrs. otherwise normal. Weather good 1 O.R. returned from Leave. RWB.	
	28th		Lt. Fryer + 2 O.R. left for a Camouflage Course. 1 O.R. returned from hospital. Situation normal. Weather good. RWB. 1 O.R. returned from Course, Camiers.	
GOUZEAUCOURT 1/20000	29th		Two Machine Guns fired in conjunction with Artillery on Targets in R2c & R2d also R15c. Situation normal. Weather good. Internal relief. 1 O.R. left for a M.G. Course at Camiers. RWB.	Ref. GOUZEAU-COURT 1/20000
	30th		Enemy Artillery busy at times. Weather good. RWB.	

A7092). Wt. W12839/M1293. 750,000. 1/17. D. D & L., Ltd. Forms/C2118/14.

Instructions regarding War Diaries and Intelligence Summaries are contained in F. S. Regs., Part II. and the Staff Manual respectively. Title pages will be prepared in manuscript.

VOLUME 17.

WAR DIARY
or
~~INTELLIGENCE SUMMARY.~~
(Erase heading not required.)

OCTOBER 1917. 120 MACHINE GUN COY.

Army Form C. 2118.

Vol 17

Place	Date Oct	Hour	Summary of Events and Information	Remarks and references to Appendices
Q12d.60.05. Ref GOUZEAUCOURT 1/20000.	1st		Weather fair. Hostile & own artillery quiet. Enemy very much on the alert at night. VILLERS-PLOVICH BEAUCAMP ROAD shelled intermittently during the day with 4.2's. 1 OR. Killed. RGF	
	2nd		Hostile Patrol seen about 20 strong in front of our wire by BROOKSBY LANE they were dispersed by M.G. & Rifle fire. 2 E.A. flew over our lines & were driven off by AA fire during the night. 2 of our M.G's engaged tracks & roads used by enemy. 4000 Rounds expended. 1 OR returned from hospital. RGF	
	3rd		1 O.R. proceeded to U.K. on leave. Hostile M.G.'s very active sweeping No mans land during the night. Enemy reported to be very alert. Hostile artillery fairly quiet. BEAUCAMP BEET FACTORY received considerable attention. Information received that 2nd & 5th armies attacked this morning on about 11,000 yards front between BITTER WOOD & N of GRAVENSTAFEL. No details received. Warning Order received stating that 40th Division would be relieved in a few days time by the 20th Division. RGF	
	4th		Hostile & own artillery activity quiet during day. but at 7 pm Enemy opened heavy bombardment on our centre & left company fronts, the shelling was exceptionally heavy near ASHBY ALLEY at (R7b 60.40). At 7.25 pm a raiding party estimated to be about 40 strong attempted to enter our trenches at about R7b 80.05. one man only getting through our wire, the remainder were driven off by our Machine Gun & rifle fire, one prisoner being left in our hands. One of our gun team slightly wounded by a fragment of a bomb, our Machine Gun fired 1700 Rounds. Prisoner belonged to 107 Pioneer Coy. 54th Division.	
			Our Machine Guns fired on RANCOURT FARM ROAD & gaps in enemies wire during the hours of darkness. 1 O.R admitted to hospital, 1 OR returned from hospital. Sergt-Amos transferred to 173 M G Coy to assume duty as C.S.M. RGF	

A7092). Wt. W12839/M1293 750,000. 1/17. D. D & L., Ltd. Forms/C2118/14.

Army Form C. 2118.

Instructions regarding War Diaries and Intelligence Summaries are contained in F. S. Regs., Part II. and the Staff Manual respectively. Title pages will be prepared in manuscript.

VOLUME 17.

WAR DIARY
or
~~INTELLIGENCE~~ SUMMARY.
(Erase heading not required.)

OCTOBER 1917

120 MACHINE GUN COY.

Place	Date	Hour	Summary of Events and Information	Remarks and references to Appendices
Q12d.60.05 Ref GOUZEAUCOURT 1-20000	OCT. 5th		Left Battalion Centre Brigade carried out a raid on Enemies trenches at R15.C.9.5. supported by a Machine Gun & Artillery Barrage. 20 prisoners were captured but a certain amount of material damage caused & several of the enemy killed. 120 Machine Gun Coy relieved by 60th MACHINE GUN Coy. Company returned to huts in HEUDECOURT. 4 OR returned from	
HEUDECOURT.			Divisional Signalling Course. 2/Lt H.A.R. THOMPSON & 1 OR admitted to Convalescent hospital. RJG	
	6th		Weather bad, rained all day. Company entrained at HEUDECOURT and moved into huts in PERONNE. RJG	
PERONNE.	7th		Church Parades. 1 OR to Cookery Course ALBERT.	
	8th		Preparing to move to billets in BERNEVILLE. Cleaning & overhauling Guns & equipment. 2.30 120th Inf/Brigade inspected by G.O.C. 3rd Corps in PERONNE SQUARE. RJG Weather fair. RJG	
	9th		Brigade entrain at PERONNE and move to BOISLEUX AU MONT, then marched into Billets at BERNEVILLE & SIMENCOURT. 1 OR from Brigade hospital. RJG	
BERNEVILLE	10th		120 MACHINE GUN Coy arrived at BERNEVILLE, billeted in Huts & Barns. 40th DIVISION become part of VII Corps in army Reserve. Weather wet. RJG	
	11th		Company commenced training, about 2 hours a day to be devoted to Recreational Training. RJG	
	12th		Training carried out as per programme but owing to wet weather most of the work had to be done under cover. 6 OR returned to Base as inefficient. RJG	

A7092). Wt. W12839/M1293 750,000. 1/17. D. D & L., Ltd. Forms/C2118/14.

Army Form C. 2118.

WAR DIARY
or
~~INTELLIGENCE~~ SUMMARY.
(Erase heading not required.)

Instructions regarding War Diaries and Intelligence Summaries are contained in F. S. Regs., Part II. and the Staff Manual respectively. Title pages will be prepared in manuscript.

VOLUME 17

OCTOBER 1917

120 MACHINE GUN COY

Place	Date	Hour	Summary of Events and Information	Remarks and references to Appendices
	OCT			
BERNEVILLE	13th		Weather fine. Company Training, elementary Battery machine gun drill. 6 OR sent back to Base as inefficient. 1 OR evacuated sick. RJL	
	14th		Weather fine. Church Parades. RJL	
	15th		Advanced training commenced. Gun drill practiced with gas helmets. 1 OR proceeded to Grantham on special course. RJL	
	16th		Weather fair. Range practices carried out including firing with Box Respirators. RJL	
	17th		Bombing practice, framing reports etc, 4 extra men being trained as signallers for the new machine gun battery tactics. 1 OR returned from leave. RJL	
	18th		Weather wet. Training carried out. Recreational training during afternoon. 1 OR admitted to hospital sick. RJL	
	19th		Company Route march, weather changeable. 1 OR proceeded to UK on leave. RJL	
	20th		Company on Range all day, 16 guns used, pack animals practised, result satisfactory. 3 OR sent to Rest Camp. 1 OR evacuated sick. RJL	
	21st		Weather wet. Church Parades. RJL	
	22nd		Advanced training in tactics, trench warfare. 1 section attached to 14th HLI for tactical scheme, practised moving guns forward during an advance & consolidating positions gained. RJL	
	23rd		Advanced training continued at Trench System WAILLY, one section attached to 13th E. Surrey Regt, weather stormy. 10 Reinforcements reported from Base. 1 OR admitted to hospital. RJL	

A7092). Wt. W12839/M1293 750,000. 1/17. D. D & L., Ltd. Forms/C2118/14.

Instructions regarding War Diaries and Intelligence Summaries are contained in F. S. Regs., Part II. and the Staff Manual respectively. Title pages will be prepared in manuscript.

VOLUME 17

WAR DIARY
or
~~INTELLIGENCE SUMMARY.~~
(Erase heading not required.)

Army Form C. 2118.

OCTOBER 1917 — 120 MACHINE GUN COY.

Place	Date	Hour	Summary of Events and Information	Remarks and references to Appendices
BERNEVILLE	24th		Company Training. 1 Section attached for Tactical scheme to 14 A&SH. 1 OR to join Cadet Unit in U.K. 1 officer (2/Lt de Pelham) and one OR to days course at School of cookery Albert. RJG	
	25th		Company proceeded to WAILLY Training area carried out Tactical Scheme Battery drill, moving forward guns, choice of positions etc. RJG	
	26th		Company Route March. 1 Section attached to 14th A&SH ~~[illegible]~~ & 13th E Surreys for Tactical Scheme. Warning Order received that 40th Div would move into GHQ Reserve to 3rd or 5th Armies. RJG	
	27th		Company Training, weather wet. 2 OR's Evacuated sick. RJG	
	28th		Orders received that Brigade would entrain on 29th, Later Order postponed, Church parades, packing limbers etc ready for move. 1 OR to Base for dental treatment. RJG	
POMERA	29th		Company moved into billets at POMERA by march route weather fair, roads good. 1 OR to UK on leave. RJG	
	30th		Weather changeable. Company parades, general cleaning up etc. RJG Leave allotment shows 54 vacancies for this Company for month of November. RJG	
	31st		Company Route March. Company moves into billets at WARLINCOURT. RJG	

R J Gruyer Lt
for O.C. 120 M.G. Coy

A7092). Wt. W12839/M1293 750,000. 1/17. D. D & L., Ltd. Forms/C2118/14.

Instructions regarding War Diaries and Intelligence Summaries are contained in F. S. Regs., Part II. and the Staff Manual respectively. Title pages will be prepared in manuscript.

VOLUME 18

WAR DIARY
or
~~INTELLIGENCE~~ SUMMARY.
(Erase heading not required.)

Army Form C. 2118.

Vol 18

NOVEMBER 1917. 120 MACHINE GUN COY

Place	Date	Hour	Summary of Events and Information	Remarks and references to Appendices
WALINCOURT	Nov 1st		Coy training. 1 Off & 2 OR proceeded to U.K. on leave. RSF	
	2nd		Route march. Gun Drill. 3 OR on leave to UK. 1 OR from leave. 1 OR to Course (Artificer). RSF	
	3rd		Tactical Scheme. Machine Guns in open Warfare. 3 OR on leave. 1 OR evacuated. RSF	
	4th		Church Parades. 2 OR on leave. RSF	
	5th		Weather bad. Company training, combined gun drill. 1 OR reinforcement. 3 OR to U.K. on leave. RSF	
	6th		Weather changeable. Company Route march. Recreational training. 4 OR reinforcements from Base. 2 OR on leave. 1 Off & 2 OR to M.G. Course Camiers. RSF	
	7th		Weather wet. Gas Helmet drill & Stoppages. Machine Gun Lectures. 2 OR to UK on leave. RSF	
	8th		Company Scheme. Advanced Guards. Immediate Action. 1 OR to UK on leave. 2/Lt THOMPSON evacuated whilst in hospital. Surplus to establishment. RSF	
	9th		Tactical Scheme Machine Guns in open fighting. 2 OR on leave. RSF	
	10th		Rear Guard Actions. use of Machine Guns. O.C. on Brigade Staff Ride. 2 OR to U.K. on leave. RSF	
	11th		Church Parades. 1 OR on leave. RSF	

A7092). Wt. W12839/M1293 750,000. 1/17. D. D & L., Ltd. Forms/C2118/14.

VOLUME 18

Instructions regarding War Diaries and Intelligence Summaries are contained in F. S. Regs., Part II. and the Staff Manual respectively. Title pages will be prepared in manuscript.

WAR DIARY
or
INTELLIGENCE SUMMARY.
(Erase heading not required.)

Army Form C. 2118.

NOVEMBER 1917. 120th Machine Gun Company

Place	Date	Hour	Summary of Events and Information	Remarks and references to Appendices
WALINCOURT	12/11/17		Coy training. Firing on Range. 1 Off + 1 OR to UK on leave. 1 Off to Hosp. 1 OR from leave. 1 OR from Hos. C7 L de P	
"	13/11/17		Coy on manoeuvres with 120th Infy Bde Inspected by F.M. Sir Douglas Haig. 1 Off to UK on leave. 1 OR from Hosp. C7 L de P	
"	14/11/17		Coy training. Firing on Range. 1 OR to UK on leave. 1 OR to Hosp. C7 L de P	
"	15/11/17		Coy training. Overhauling and cleaning of guns + equipment. 1 L/Sgt + 1 Cpl to UK for Course. C7 L de P	
WALINCOURT + BERNEVILLE	16/11/17		Coy moved into billets at Berneville, weather fine roads good. Left WALINCOURT 4-50am arrived BERNEVILLE 1 pm. C7 L de P	
BERNEVILLE + COURCELLES LE COMTE	17/11/17		Coy moved into billets at COURCELLES LE COMTE by night. Started at 7-30 pm arrived COURCELLES LE COMTE at 12-50 am 18/11/17. 1 O.R. to U.K. on leave. C7 L de P	
COURCELLES LE COMTE	18/11/17		Coy at rest. Inspection of equipment. 1 Off + 1 O.R. from leave. 1 OR accidentally hurt (evacuated) C7 L de P	
" " " "	19/11/17		Coy moved from COURCELLES LE COMTE to BOULENCOURT by day. 1 OR to UK on leave. C7 L de P	
BOULENCOURT	20/11/17		Coy at rest. Drawing of equipment + clothing. 2 OR from leave. C7 L de P	
" " "	21/11/17		Coy moved from BOULENCOURT to LEBUQUERIE. 3 OR from leave. 1 OR to A.G.C. Details to Camp "A" BOURLENCOURT. C7 L de P	
LEBUQUERIE	22/11/17		Coy moved from LEBUQUERIE to HINDERBURG SUPPORT LINE S.W. of GRANCOURT. 1 OR from leave. C7 L de P	
In the Field	23/11/17		Coy moved to shelters N.E. of GRANCOURT in sunken road. 6 OR from leave. 1 OR from Hos. 1 Off accidentally injured. C7 L de P	
" " "	24/11/17		Coy took up position S.W. of BOURLON WOOD and prepared S.O.S. barrage. 1 O.R. wounded. 1 OR to Hosp. 2 OR evacuated. C7 L de P	
" " "	25/11/17 + 26/11/17		Coy standing to for S.O.S. 1 OR wounded. 3 O.R. from leave. Details move to TRESCAULT. C7 L de P	
" " "	27/11/17		At 6.20 am. Coy opened fire on barrage lines to support attack launched by 62nd Division on BOURLON VILLAGE. Massed formations of enemy were dispersed with heavy casualties. at 2-10 pm. a strong party of enemy were dispersed by our fire, who were enfilading positions, from a disabled tank. C7 L de P	

A7092). Wt. W12839/M1293. 750,000. 1/17. D. D & L., Ltd. Forms/C2118/14.

VOLUME 18

Army Form C. 2118.

WAR DIARY
or
INTELLIGENCE SUMMARY.
(Erase heading not required.)

Instructions regarding War Diaries and Intelligence Summaries are contained in F. S. Regs., Part II. and the Staff Manual respectively. Title pages will be prepared in manuscript.

NOVEMBER 1917 — 120th Machine Gun Company

Place	Date	Hour	Summary of Events and Information	Remarks and references to Appendices
In the Field	24/11/17		Evacuated positions at 4 pm and moved to trenches in HINDERBURG SUPPORT LINE S.W. of GRANCOURT C.F.L.de P.	
" " "	28/11/17		Coy moved to billets in Blairville by Bus via Havrincourt Metz & Bapaume. 1 OR to Hosp, 2 OR from Leave C.F.L.de P.	
" " "	29/11/17		Coy overhauling & cleaning kits, rifles & clothing 2 Off + 5 OR from Leave. C.F.L.de P.	
" " "	30/11/17		Coy on parade overhauling & cleaning of guns, equipment & limbers C.F.L.de P.	

30/11/17

C. F. L. de Pelham 2nd Lieut
for O.C.
120th M. G. Coy

A7092). Wt. W12839/M1293. 750,000. 1/17. D. D & L., Ltd. Forms/C2118/14.

31/12/17

H. Q.
120th Inf. Bde

Herewith War Diary Volume 19 for December 1917

120 MACHINE GUN COY.
Number G.O. 31.12.17
Date ....

[illegible] Lt.
for O/C 120th M.G.C.

Instructions regarding War Diaries and Intelligence Summaries are contained in F. S. Regs., Part II. and the Staff Manual respectively. Title pages will be prepared in manuscript.

VOLUME 19

DECEMBER 1917

WAR DIARY
or
INTELLIGENCE SUMMARY.
(*Erase heading not required.*)

Vol 19

Army Form C. 2118.

120th Machine Gun Company

Place	Date	Hour	Summary of Events and Information	Remarks and references to Appendices
BUTMENTS HENDECOURT-LEZ-RANZART (LENS 11 1/100000 I IV)	1.12.17		Division out of the line. Company Parades. 1 OR. from leave; 10 reinforcements from Base Depot. 1OR to hospital. Cold & Windy	
	2.12.17		Division in line; Brigade at rest. Church Parade. All belts & belt boxes handed over to 119 M.G Coy. 2 OR. evacuated from Hospital. Very windy; cold at night.	
	3.12.17		Company move to MOYNEVILLE by road. Brigade relieves 119th Brigade in Reserve to Division. Two officers reconnoitre routes to left & right Brigades & thence to line in case of emergency. Lt Sharpe & 1 OR rejoin from hospital; 1OR from Course; 1OR from leave. Showery; milder.	
MOYNE CAMP MOYENNEVILLE (LENS 11 1/100000 J IV)	4.12.17		OC & 4 officers reconnoitre left Brigade Sector. 120 Belt Boxes drawn. Company prepare for line. Company move into line under tactical control 121st Brigade in FONTAINE sector – front from U1a 30.65 to U14a 70.20. Eight guns 240th & eight guns 101st M.G Coys relieved. Disposition:– FARMERS LANE, 12 guns; T17B 95.90, 4 guns. Company HQ 93 SHAFT TRENCH. 1OR from leave. 1OR to hospital; 3OR to U.K on leave. Wind drops; frost at night.	TRENCH MAP BULLECOURT 51B SW4
93 SHAFT TRENCH T6a 30.70	5.12.17		VI Corps memorandum considers it possible Enemy will endeavour to regain old positions in HINDENBURG LINE for winter. Orders issued to sentries to be particularly vigilant. Hostile artillery and E.A. active – bombs dropped on back areas. 4OR to U.K on leave. Fair & cold.	
	6.12.17		Hostile artillery quiet. Six EA high over our lines to-day. Work done on new positions A15, T5d 80.85. 2/Lt Thomas & 3OR from M.G Course Camiers; 1OR from leave. 1OR evacuated from Hospital; 3OR to U.K on leave; 1OR to M.G Course Camiers. Cold wind; hard frost at night	
	7.12.17		Hostile Artillery quiet. Aerial activity small. Work done at A15. Lt Sharpe & 2OR to U.K on leave. Fair & cold; frost at night. Rum used in absence of glycerine to prevent water in guns freezing. Found to be quite efficient	
	8.12.17		Slight hostile artillery activity. Hostile Air activity – nil. Two guns moved from FARMERS LANE to A15. 3OR to U.K on leave. Milder, slight drizzle during day	

Instructions regarding War Diaries and Intelligence Summaries are contained in F. S. Regs., Part II. and the Staff Manual respectively. Title pages will be prepared in manuscript.

VOLUME 19

DECEMBER 1917

WAR DIARY
or
INTELLIGENCE SUMMARY.
(*Erase heading not required.*)

120th Machine Gun Company

Army Form C. 2118.

Place	Date	Hour	Summary of Events and Information	Remarks and references to Appendices
Q. SHAFT TRENCH	9.12.17		Very little enemy artillery fire. No aeroplanes over our lines. 2 OR. to U.K on leave; 1 OR evacuated from hospital. Cold ?	
T6a 30.70 (TRENCH MAP BULLECOURT 51B S.W.4)	10.12.17		Divisional memo. refers to possibility of surprise attack on this front similar to enemy attack of 30.11.17. Brigade orders that stand to shall last from 1½ hrs before dawn to 2 hrs after daylight. 120 M.G. Coy relieves 121 M.G. Coy; 120 Brigade relieves 121st Brigade. Company's guns disposed:- FIT LANE, No 4 Sec; POM ALLEY No 2 Sec; FARMERS LANE and A15 No 3 Sec; QUARRY No 1 Sec, Company HQ. ST. LEGER. Six guns of 121 M.G. Coy remain in line. Increased enemy artillery activity. Enemy aeroplanes active. One O.R to U.K on leave; one O.R to hospital. Some wind; mild. At 12 midnight remaining 10 guns of 121st M.G. Coy reinforce line occupying our old positions in FARMERS LANE	BULLECOURT 51B SW 4 TRENCH MAP
ST. LEGER	11.12.17		Enemy Artillery & Aircraft active. One OR to U.K on leave. One from Course. Fine; mild.	
	12.12.17	3-4am	4 Guns fired 10,000 rounds on possible enemy assembly points in No man's land	
		6.30am	Enemy make local attack on 3rd Brigade of 3rd Division on our right. Enemy barrage falls on our Divisional front. S.O.S sent up from our right Brigade. 30,000 rounds fired by Coy's guns on S.O.S lines. 1 Gun at QUARRY knocked out; 1 OR killed, 2 wounded. Our & enemy artillery and aircraft active during day — many of our 'planes over our lines. At 6.35 am. New positions for Quarry guns reconnoitred by O.C. Weather mild; no wind.	

A7092). Wt. W12839/M1293 750,000. 1/17. D. D & L., Ltd. Forms/C2118/14.

Instructions regarding War Diaries and Intelligence Summaries are contained in F. S. Regs., Part II, and the Staff Manual respectively. Title pages will be prepared in manuscript.

VOLUME 19

WAR DIARY
or
INTELLIGENCE SUMMARY.
(Erase heading not required.)

Army Form C. 2118.

DECEMBER 1917 — 120th Machine Gun Company

Place	Date	Hour	Summary of Events and Information	Remarks and references to Appendices
ST. LEGER.	13.12.17	12 MN DAWN	Coy. Guns fired 7500 rounds on "no mans land" in vicinity of Lucon BRIDGE. The Guns at Quarry moved one at a time, to new positions at T.R.C 46.30 after dusk. Gas shelling by enemy from 12 noon to 1 pm and again from 10.30pm to midnight, in the neighbourhood of [illegible] ALLEY. Harassing fire from 2 Guns on FONTAINE VILLAGE and WOOD 10PM – 12 MN. Hostile Artillery fairly quiet. Hostile aerial activity Nil. DULL MILD.	
	14.12.17	12 MN. DAWN	One Gun fired 3500 rounds on No-Mans Land.	
		3.45 to 4.45	Two Guns fired in cooperation with 121 M.G. Coy. One O.R. slightly wounded (remained at duty). Hostile aerial activity very quiet. Mild Dull.	
	15.12.17	12 MN. to 2 AM	Company guns fired as follows: Harassing fire on FONTAINE VILLAGE and WOOD in cooperation with raid by 3rd Div on our left at 3 pm onwards.	
		6 pm.	onwards. After discharge of gas by us against the enemy on our front 12000 rds harassing fire. 1 O.R. killed and 2/Lt Bennett wounded. Hostile artillery quiet. E.A. activity nil. Bright and cold.	
	16.12.17		Hostile artillery quiet. E.A. activity nil. One O.R. leave to U.K. Cold dull, snow at night.	
	17.12.17		Enemy shelled our front line system lightly during day. E.A. activity nil. One O.R. to U.K on leave. One O.R. from leave. Snow on ground. Dull, thawed during afternoon.	
	18.12.17		120 Inf Bde relieved by 121 Inf Bde. Coy remained in line. During night Company's guns fired 35,000 rounds in cooperation with artillery. Increased hostile artillery fire. Hostile air activity nil. One O.R admitted to hospital. One O.R. from leave. Colder, Keen frost at night.	
	19.12.17		Company relieved by 121st M.G.C and moved to MOYNE CAMP MOYNEVILLE. Six guns of 120th M.G.C remain in line attached to 121st M.G.C occupy Corps positions. 1 O.R. to U.K on leave.	

Army Form C. 2118.

VOLUME 19

WAR DIARY
or
INTELLIGENCE SUMMARY.
(Erase heading not required.)

Instructions regarding War Diaries and Intelligence Summaries are contained in F. S. Regs., Part II. and the Staff Manual respectively. Title pages will be prepared in manuscript.

DECEMBER 1917 — 120th Machine Gun Company

Place	Date	Hour	Summary of Events and Information	Remarks and references to Appendices
MOYNE CAMP MOYNEVILLE	20.12.17		The Company at rest. Gun Kit overhauled and new clothes issued to men. Men have baths. 20 O.R. admitted to hospital. 1 O.R. from leave	
	21.12.17		Inspection of Company by O.C. of iron rations and box respirators. Route march. 7 O.R. admitted to Hospital suffering from slight fevers. One O.R. to U.K on leave.	
	22.12.17		Six guns in Corps line relieved by six from Details. Christmas dinner to N.C.Os and men. One O.R. admitted to Hospital. One O.R. to U.K on leave. Two O.R. from leave. One O.R. from Hospital.	
	23.12.17		Church Parades. Company prepares for line. One O.R. admitted to Hospital. One O.R. rejoins from Hospital. Christmas dinner sent to teams in line. Lt Phillips joined Coy from 14th M.G.C.	
ST LEGER	24.12.17		Company relieve 121st M.G. Coy in line — all 121st go out of line. Line guns disposed as follows:- FIT LANE, POM ALLEY, FARMERS LANE, A15 QUARRY and FACTORY. Two guns each on S.O.S and BATTLE lines. Four guns T17C 30.60 T17C 18.75 T17d 95.15 and T17d 50.30 together with two FACTORY guns remain in Corps line. Enemy Artillery quiet. No enemy air activity	
	25.12.17		Christmas Day. A very quiet day, with little activity of any kind. Today the keen frost of the last six days breaks.	
	26.12.17		A quiet day, with little activity of any kind. One O.R. from leave and 8 reinforcements from 121st M.G.C. Bright & cold.	
MOYNE CAMP	27.12.17		Company relieved by 101st M.G.C. and move to MOYNE CAMP. Everything quiet and in order. Bright & cold. Lt Tams ~~on~~ to U.K on leave.	

(A7092). Wt. W12839/M1293. 750,000. 1/17. D. D. & L., Ltd. Forms/C.2118/14.

Instructions regarding War Diaries and Intelligence Summaries are contained in F. S. Regs., Part II. and the Staff Manual respectively. Title pages will be prepared in manuscript.

VOLUME 19

VOLUME 19

DECEMBER

DECEMBER 1917

WAR DIARY
or
INTELLIGENCE SUMMARY.
(Erase heading not required.)

120th Machine Gun Company

Place	Date	Hour	Summary of Events and Information	Remarks and references to Appendices
NOREUIL	28.12.17		Company relieved the 8th M.G.C. 3rd Div in the ~~NOREUIL~~ NOREUIL sector. Guns disposed as follows. No 15, 22/1, 22/2, 21/1, 21/2, 22/A, 20/A, ~~F5~~ X and Y batteries, No 24 and 25. All guns on S.O.S. and battle lines. Enemy artillery quiet. Air activity Nil. One O.R. from leave. One O.R. on leave to U.K. Very cold & windy.	
	29.12.17		A quiet day with little activity of any kind. Guns fired 2000 rounds on enemy C.Ts and roads. One O.R. on leave to U.K. Cold and dull.	
	30.12.17		A quiet day. X Battery fired 2000 rounds on U 23 a 00.40. Also Y battery fired on OSTRICH and BULL DOG AVENUES. 1 O.R. leave to U.K. Cold dull.	
	31.12.17		Quiet day. A few enemy shells in neighbourhood of SYDNEY AVENUE. X Machine gun battery fired 2000 rounds during night on enemy C.Ts at U 23 A. 00 40. 1 O.R. (accidentally) wounded. 1 O.R. leave to U.K. Lieut A. DUNCAN and 2/Lt E. LIGHT joined the Coy from M.G. Base. Cold and dull.	

30.12.17

[signature]
for O.C.
120th M.G. Coy

(A7092). Wt. W12839/M1293. 750,000. 1/17. D. D. & L., Ltd. Forms/C.2118/14.

VOLUME 20

Army Form C. 2118.

Instructions regarding War Diaries and Intelligence Summaries are contained in F. S. Regs., Part II. and the Staff Manual respectively. Title pages will be prepared in manuscript.

WAR DIARY
or
INTELLIGENCE SUMMARY.
(Erase heading not required.)

JANUARY 1918 120th Machine Gun Company.

Vol 20

Place	Date	Hour	Summary of Events and Information	Remarks and references to Appendices
MOREUIL	1-1-18		Fairly quiet day. Hostile Artillery active during morning also E.A. Fine & cold. 2 R.Os to Hospital	
	2.1.18		Quiet day. Situation normal. Dull and thawing.	
	3.1.18		Situation normal. Hostile activity active during night. No wounded. Cold. 1 O.R. on leave	
	4.1.18		Quiet day. During night of Friday–Saturday Company's Guns fired 13,000 rounds on S.O.S. lines. Cold and dull.	
	5.1.18		Day quiet. Situation normal. During night Guns fired 17,000 rounds on various targets, S.O.S. having gone up. Situation cleared by 7.15 AM. Cold and bright.	
	6.1.18		Hostile Artillery and E.A. activity very quiet. 1 O.R. leave to U.K. – Cold and Dull.	
	7.1.18		Enemy put down Barrage on front line from 6.30 AM to 7.30 AM and again from 4.30 PM to 5.15 pm. Aviation quiet. M.Gs fired 15,000 rds on [illegible] lines from 6–9 AM. 1 O.R. leave to U.K. Clear.	
	8.1.18		Hostile Artillery and E.A. quiet. M.Gs fired 2500 rounds harassing fire on enemy lines of communication. 1 O.R. leave U.K.	
	9.1.18		Hostile Artillery very active at dawn. At 9.45 am 2 E.A. attempted to cross our lines but were driven back by M.G. fire. This was repeated between 9 AM and 10 AM. 1 O.R. leave U.K. – Dull and misty.	

Instructions regarding War Diaries and Intelligence Summaries are contained in F. S. Regs., Part II. and the Staff Manual respectively. Title pages will be prepared in manuscript.

VOL 20

WAR DIARY
or
INTELLIGENCE SUMMARY.
(Erase heading not required.)

Army Form C. 2118.

JANUARY 1918 — [illegible] Machine Gun [illegible]

Place	Date	Hour	Summary of Events and Information	Remarks and references to Appendices
[illegible]	[illegible]		[illegible]	
	[illegible]		[illegible]	
	[illegible]		[illegible]	
	[illegible]		[illegible]	
	[illegible]		[illegible]	
	[illegible]		[illegible]	[illegible] Appendix No. 2
			[illegible]	
DYSART CAMP ERVILLERS	[illegible]		[illegible]	
	[illegible]		[illegible]	
	[illegible]		[illegible]	
	[illegible]		[illegible]	

A7092). Wt. W12839/M1293 750,000. 1/17. D. D & L., Ltd. Forms/C2118/14.

VOL 20

WAR DIARY
or
INTELLIGENCE SUMMARY.
(Erase heading not required.)

Army Form C. 2118.

Instructions regarding War Diaries and Intelligence Summaries are contained in F. S. Regs., Part II. and the Staff Manual respectively. Title pages will be prepared in manuscript.

JANUARY 1918 [illegible]

Place	Date	Hour	Summary of Events and Information	Remarks and references to Appendices
[illegible]	[illegible]		[illegible] 1 OR leave UK [illegible]	
	[illegible]		[illegible]	
			1 OR leave UK 1 OR returned from leave [illegible]	
[illegible]	[illegible]		[illegible] CAPT [illegible] OLIVER-THOMPSON [illegible] 2nd LT [illegible] command and LT [illegible] 1 OR leave UK 1 OR returned from leave	
	[illegible]		[illegible]	
	[illegible]		[illegible] NOREUIL [illegible] 1 OR leave UK 1 OR returned from leave. [illegible]	
	[illegible]		[illegible] Misty. 1 OR from leave, 1 OR to UK on leave [illegible]	
	27.1.18		Artillery quiet during day. At 8 pm an Artillery test S.O.S. was fired in co-operation with Division on Right. Machine Guns fired one belt per gun on S.O.S. lines. From 10.15 to 10.45 hostile artillery bombarded NOREUIL, DEWSBURY TRENCH, large proportion of gas shells used. Misty. 1 OR from leave. 1 OR to UK on leave; 4 O.R. evacuated sick	

A7092). Wt. W12839/M1293 750,000. 1/17. D. D & L., Ltd. Forms/C2118/14.

Army Form C. 2118.

VOLUME 20

WAR DIARY
or
INTELLIGENCE SUMMARY.
(*Erase heading not required.*)

Instructions regarding War Diaries and Intelligence Summaries are contained in F. S. Regs., Part II. and the Staff Manual respectively. Title pages will be prepared in manuscript.

JANUARY 1918

125th Machine Gun Company.

Place	Date	Hour	Summary of Events and Information	Remarks and references to Appendices
NOREUIL	28.1.18		Our artillery & aircraft active. Hostile aircraft active, artillery generally quiet. 1OR from leave, 1OR from hospital, 1OR to hospital. Bright, frost at night [initials]	2/Lt Pelham to U.K. on leave [initials]
	29.1.18		Artillery & aircraft on both sides, considerable activity of. Enemy aircraft bombed back areas during night. 1OR on leave; 1OR from leave. Bright, frost at night. [initials]	
	30.1.18		Our & hostile Artillery Active – concentration fired by our artillery on new trench U.10.d 05.38 to U16.b 32.65 from 10am to 10.30 am. Hostile aircraft active. Bright, frost at night. 1OR from leave. One OR reinforcement. One OR to U.K. on leave [initials]	
	31.1.18		Quiet day. One OR to U.K. on leave. Foggy & cold with frost at night [initials]	

A7092). Wt. W12839/M1295 750,000. 1/17. D. D & L., Ltd. Forms/C2118/14.

VOLUME 21.

WAR DIARY
or
INTELLIGENCE SUMMARY.

Army Form C. 2118.

Instructions regarding War Diaries and Intelligence Summaries are contained in F. S. Regs., Part II. and the Staff Manual respectively. Title pages will be prepared in manuscript.

(Erase heading not required.)

FEBRUARY 1918. 120th Machine Gun Company.

Place	Date	Hour	Summary of Events and Information	Remarks and references to Appendices
NOREUIL	1-2-18		Very slight enemy shelling. Very quiet. Very cold and dull all day. 1 O.R. on leave. 2 O.R. from leave. 1 O.R. from Hospital. C.F. [illegible]	
"	2-2-18		Enemy artillery and aircraft very quiet. Clear and bright, cold and frosty at night. 1 O.R. on leave. C.F. [illegible]	
"	3-2-18		Hostile artillery active & aircraft alert. Bursts of E Mac Gun fire sweeping Railway Reserve. Warm, light clouds with occasional sunshine. C.F. [illegible]	
"	4-2-18		Enemy artillery very active with occasional bombardments of 15 minutes duration. E.A. normal. Warm, light clouds. 8 Reinforcements reported. 1 O.R. from leave. 1 O.R. on leave. 2 O.R. to Hospital. C.F. [illegible]	
"	5-2-18		Enemy artillery quieter. 8 Observation balloons were observed in the morning. E.A. normal. Mild, Dull. No sun. 1 O.R. on leave. 1 O.R. from leave. 1 O.R. to Hospital. C.F. [illegible]	
"	6-2-18		Enemy artillery quiet and also E.A. 1 machine (nationality unknown) came down in flames. 1 O.R. on leave. 2 O.R. from leave. 1 O.R. from Hospital. 2 O.R.s to Hospital. Mild, sunshine at intervals. C.F. [illegible]	
"	7-2-18		Intermittent hostile artillery shelling. E.A. not seen all day. Mild, drizzling rain morning and evening. 1 O.R. from leave. 1 O.R. on leave. 2 O.R. from Courses. 1 O.R. to Hospital. C.F. [illegible]	
"	8-2-18		Enemy artillery normal. Single E.A. came over lines in morning. Dull with slight drizzle. 1 O.R. on leave. 1 O.R. off strength. C.F. [illegible]	
"	9-2-18		Support lines shelled with Enemy Trench Mortars. No E.A. seen. Bright and clear, mild. [illegible] Light on leave. 6 Mac Guns concentrated on Starfish Trench, in consequence of gas projectors having been reported placed there. C.F. [illegible]	
"	10-2-18		Enemy artillery quiet also E.A. Warm and clear. 1 Officer on Course & 1 O.R. C.F. [illegible]	
"	11-2-18		Enemy artillery more active, E.A. normal. Warm and clear. 1 O.R. on leave. At 4.30 pm relieved by 14th Mac Gun Coy and Coy on relief marched back to billets at DURROW CAMP MORY. Relief very good. C.F. [illegible]	

(A7092) Wt. W12839/M1293. 750,000. 1/17. D. D. & L., Ltd. Forms/C.2118/14.

VOLUME 21

Army Form C. 2118.

Instructions regarding War Diaries and Intelligence Summaries are contained in F. S. Regs., Part II. and the Staff Manual respectively. Title pages will be prepared in manuscript.

WAR DIARY
or
INTELLIGENCE SUMMARY.
(Erase heading not required.)

February 1918 — 120th Machine Gun Company

Place	Date	Hour	Summary of Events and Information	Remarks and references to Appendices
DORROW CAMP, MORY.	12-2-18		Coy paraded 10am and marched to No 6 Camp HENDECOURT-LEZ-RANSART. Warm and clear. 1 OR on leave 2 OR's from leave 1 OR to Hospital. G.H. det	
HENDECOURT LEZ RANSART	13-2-18		Coy paraded 9am to clean up camp and limbers. Major ROBERTS M.C., O.C. 40th Div M.G. Battn. arrived and joined Mess. Raining all day. 1 OR on leave 1 OR from leave 2 OR to Hospital. G.H. det	
"	1412-18		Coy paraded at 9am and moved to No 4 Camp HENDECOURT-LEZ-RANSART except Transport. 2/Lieut. PELHAM from leave. 1 OR to leave. 1 OR on Course 1 OR from Hospital. Wet and drizzling all day. Camp in very dirty condition, afternoon spent in cleaning up Camp. G.H. det	
"	15-2-18		Coy paraded at 9am cleaning up camp all day. 1 OR on leave. 1 OR attached. Dull and dry. G.H. det	
"	16-2-18		Coy paraded 8.30am Inspection by Major ROBERTS M.C. remainder of morning cleaning Camp and Limbers. 1 OR on leave 1 OR from leave. Cold and bright. Some frost at night. 1 OR evacuated. G.H. det	
"	17-2-18		O.C. Coy and Section Officers reconnoitred Reserve Positions ~~in~~ ST LEGER and BOYELLES Sectors. Company cleaning Limbers and Camp morning and afternoon. Cold and bright. 2 OR's from leave 1 OR on leave. G.H. det	
"	18-2-18		Company training. Inspection of Transport by G.O.C. 40th Division, Company complimented. Clear and bright. 1 OR on leave. 1 OR from Hospital 1 OR evacuated 2 Reinforcement from 14th H.L.I. and 9 from 13th E. Surrey Regt. G.H. det	
"	19-2-18		Company moved at 10am to ENNISKILLEN CAMP, ERVILLERS. Cold and bright. 1 OR on leave 1 OR from leave 1 OR from Hospital. G.H. det	
ERVILLERS.	20-2-18		Company paraded for cleaning up Camp. Dull and drizzling. 1 OR from leave. 1 OR on leave	G.H. det

VOLUME 21

Instructions regarding War Diaries and Intelligence Summaries are contained in F. S. Regs., Part II. and the Staff Manual respectively. Title pages will be prepared in manuscript.

WAR DIARY
or
INTELLIGENCE SUMMARY.
(Erase heading not required.)

Army Form C. 2118.

February 1918 — 120th Machine Gun Company

Place	Date	Hour	Summary of Events and Information	Remarks and references to Appendices
ERVILLERS	21-2-18		Cleaning up camp by company 1 OR on leave 1 OR from leave. Bright and clear. C.H.L. de P.	
"	22-2-18		Company paraded till 11 am for Drill and rest of morning on fatigue. Dry fine and bright. 9 Reinforcements from A & S Highlanders. 1 OR on leave. C.H.L. de P.	
"	23-2-18		Company bathed and rest of morning cleaning up camp. Dull very mild. 1 OR on leave. 1 OR from leave 1 OR on course. C.H.L. de P.	
"	24-2-18		Company paraded for Church. Dull occasional shower. 1 OR on leave. 1 OR from leave 1 OR from Hospital. 5 ORs evacuated. C.H.L. de P.	
"	25-2-18		Company cleaning up camp and Huts for G.O.C. 40th Division Inspection at 2-30 pm. Company complimented. Stormy windy and raining. 1 OR on leave. 1 OR from leave 1 OR evacuated. 1 OR from Hospital. C.H.L. de P.	
"	26-2-18		Company paraded at 9 am for Training. O.C. Company & 3 Section Officers reconnoitred positions in NEUVELLE VITASSE sector. Bright and warm. 1 OR to Hospital. 1 OR on leave. C.H.L. de P.	
"	27-2-18		Company moved to position at NEUVILLE VITASSE and relieved 119th Mac Gun Coy. Relief complete by 2-30 pm. Dry clear and bright, slight rain in evening. 2/LIEUT. LIGHT from leave 1 OR on leave. C.H.L. de P.	
"	28/2/18		Enemy artillery and aircraft quiet. Bright clear and mild. 4 ORs on leave. Capt. J. H. OLIVER THOMPSON from leave. C.H.L. de P.	

C.H. L de Pelham 2/Lt
for O.C.
"B" Coy 40th Div M. G. Batt.
(late 120 M.G. Coy)

1st March 1918.

A7092). Wt. W12839/M1293 750,000. 1/17. D. D & L., Ltd. Forms/C2118/14.

www.ingramcontent.com/pod-product-compliance
Lightning Source LLC
Chambersburg PA
CBHW081536160426
43191CB00011B/1775